The Little Earth Book

by

James Bruges

D0301184

To James' children: Ben, Clare, Kate and Bea
and to Alastair's children: Toby and Rowan

An Alastair Sawday Publishing Special

Written and researched by James Bruges
Published by Alastair Sawday Publishing
Editor: Alastair Sawday
Cover design: Caroline King
Overall design concept: Caroline King
Design: Springboard Design Partnership
Picture research and lay-out: Sam Duby
Original illustrations: Mark Brierley
Editorial advice: Rachel Fielding
Pre-production: Avonset
Printing: Midas Printing (UK) Limited

First edition 2000
Copyright © November 2000 Alastair Sawday Publishing Co. Ltd
The Home Farm, Barrow Gurney, Bristol BS48 3RW

ISBN 1-901970-23-X

Contents

5 **Introduction**

9 **Little Earth** - our only home

11 **Cod** - a symbol for our times

14 **Don't Predict!** - just be systematic

16 **Ozone Layer** - a ray of hope

18 **Carbon and Temperature** - uncharted territory

22 **Global Warming** - dealing with uncertainty

26 **Europe Cooling** - ocean currents

29 **Water** - fresh water is running out

33 **Ecological Footprints** - the rich wear big boots

35 **Inequality** - a bequest of the 20th century

38 **Weapons of War** - an environmental issue

40 **An Oxymoron?** - sustainable development

42 **Rio and Kyoto** - slow progress

44 **Trading Pollution Quotas** - a practical approach

46 **Domestic Tradable Quotas** - towards equity in each country

49 **Contraction and Convergence** - the logical step after Kyoto

52 **Making Money** - it's really quite simple

54 **Banks** - they've got you by the jugular

56 **Economic Growth** - and the second law of thermodynamics

58 **A Paradox** - the history of growth: it makes things worse

60 **Citizen's Income** - for a civilized civilization

63 **Wörgl** - money that is not worth keeping

65 **A New World Order** - four currencies

67 **"Them' or "Us"** - a Gandhian approach

70 **Wealth in Poverty** - a tribal's view

4

73 **A Great American Idea** - odious debt

75 **Third World Debt** - view from the North

78 **First World Debt** - view from the South

81 **The World Trade Organisation** - dull but important

84 **Free Trade** - winners and losers

87 **Basic Needs** - isn't everyone as happy as we are?

89 **Feeding the World** - a risky business

92 **Farming** - has it gone mad?

96 **Organics** - respecting nature's way

98 **POP!** - synthetic timebombs

101 **The Agrochemical Revolution** - was it a success?

104 **Pests and Weeds** - putting humanity at risk

107 **Controlling the Food Chain** - the terminator

110 **Microbes** - tougher than humans?

112 **Superbugs and Antibiotics** - a gift of nature rejected

114 **Genes** - and genetic experimentation

117 **Nature in Balance** - survival of the fittest?

119 **Population** - more or less?

121 **Patenting Life** - wait a minute! Who made it?

123 **Commercial Eugenics** - will life science lead us by the nose?

125 **Understanding Nature** - and redesigning life

127 **Intuition** - common sense, imagination, and morality

129 **Two Japanese Farmers** - more with less - a fascinating tale

131 **Mental Equipment** - reality beyond our grasp

133 **Some Conclusions**

135 **References**

140 **A Short Story** - of one man's impact

Introduction

Just before this book went to the printers, at the end of August 2000, the editorial of the New Scientist commented: *"Levels of carbon dioxide in the atmosphere are well on the way to those found in the Eocene period when the world was ice-free and England a steaming mangrove forest."*

Such news makes some of us deeply anxious. Others will ask what they can do. This Little Earth Book will, by shedding light on complex issues, help us to respond both constructively and creatively – rather than throw up our hands and leave responsibility to 'the experts'.

The book is about new attitudes and a change of direction, not doom and gloom. And if we say some apparently dramatic things remember that scientists – in many cases the majority of them – are saying dramatic things too. They are beseeching us to look at the evidence and DO something.

This year, 2000, the Royal Commission on Environmental Pollution advised the Government that: *"The world is now faced with a radical challenge of a totally new kind, which requires an urgent response. The concentration of carbon dioxide in the atmosphere is already higher than at any time for millions of years. There is no precedent to help us understand precisely what consequences will follow. The environmental consequences are potentially catastrophic."*

This follows consistent warnings from the scientific community. Even back in 1992 1,670 scientists, including 110 of the 138 living winners of Nobel prizes in the sciences, issued the famous 'World Scientists' Warning to Humanity'. It included these comments:

"We are fast approaching many of the Earth's limits. Current economic practices which damage the environment cannot continue. Our massive tampering could trigger unpredictable collapse of critical biological systems which are only partly understood. A great change in our stewardship of the Earth and the life on it is required if vast human misery is to be avoided and our global home on this planet is not to be irretrievably mutilated."

In 1999 the chief meteorologists of Britain and the US issued a joint letter to national newspapers in both countries, including: *"Ignoring climate change will surely be the most costly of all possible choices, for us and our children."*

But politicians, vulnerable as they are to lobby groups, are – crucially – still dragging their heels. Lawrence Summers, Secretary to the US Treasury and hugely influential in the World Bank, has said: *"There are no limits to the carrying capacity of the Earth that could bind any time in the forseeable future. The idea that we should put limits on growth because of some natural limit is a profound error."*

Throughout this book you will find reference to the World Bank, for it is a giant player on the world stage. In November 1999 its Chief Economist stunned the world by resigning. He had been consistently overruled. *"It is not just the creation of a market economy that matters"*, he said, *"but the establishment of the foundations of sustainable, equitable and democratic institutions."*

So, the scientific community is saying that we are exceeding the earth's carrying capacity, and is being heeded by the United Nations. The World Bank, the IMF and the World Trade Organisation, on the other hand, are still acting as if the world's health will improve if we all consume more.

WHO IS RIGHT? Surely we should take scientists seriously when they are almost of one voice. We also have, all of us, the evidence of our own senses. We smell the increase in pollution, see the countryside being overwhelmed by concrete, listen in vain for the song of once-familiar birds, are aware through our travels of growing inequalities, and know the futility of wealth creation for its own sake.

If the scientists are right, we face human misery on an unprecedented scale, much of it caused by the policies of the World Bank and the I.M.F. and the frenzied, headlong rush towards a globalised economy which seeks to make us all into consumers, customers and competitors. Future generations will see us as guilty of the ultimate crime against humanity: allowing our Earth's support systems to die while we enjoyed the temporary benefits of an unsustainable lifestyle.

We are NOT just consumers, customers, competitors. We are, first and last, human beings. And each one of us has enormous potential to change things. This book has stirring examples of individuals thinking, acting and dreaming up new ideas. It is a clarion call to each of us. It shows us that there is hope.

How to use this book

Dip in and out if you wish; take a subject at a time. Each chapter is short and to the point– however vast the subject – and aims to provoke you, both emotionally and intellectually. Do read further; we refer you to books that go more deeply into the subjects, though the views expressed here don't necessarily represent the views of those books.

Better still, try reading it all at one or two sittings; the ideas, held together in your memory, will form a powerful whole. For that is the strength of this book: we cannot consider these global problems in isolation. They are all linked. That is why we have boldly included chapters on economics - hardly the most seductive of subjects - with others on, say, farming and genetics, because they are far too important to leave out, as you will see.

Finally...

We think this is an important, and even serious, book; every MP will receive a copy. We also think you will enjoy reading it.

James Bruges – *author*
Alastair Sawday - *publisher*

Little Earth

our only home

It was not long ago that Victorian explorers filled European drawing rooms with artifacts from beyond the known world, and conservatories with plants that had never previously been encountered. Now there are no frontiers. Satellite photos vividly show a finite planet set in space, and we have colonised nearly all of it.

This little book draws attention to radical new thinking about the environment, the economy and the life sciences, and we hope it will provoke discussion on how to live within a closed system - the planet that we share with other creatures and are learning to love with a new desperation.

Science and technology have provided immense benefits to humankind. Yet in the last thirty years human activity has destroyed a third of the planet's 'natural wealth' and may now be creating climatic chaos. Both the achievements and the degradation are driven by an economy that has concentrated a vast majority of the world's wealth into very few hands, leaving ever increasing numbers destitute.

Prophets of doom believe that we are not capable of sustaining a world that we have filled and which we now try to manage. They predict catastrophe within 40 to 80 years given recent trends. These dire forecasts assume that we will not deviate from our present suicidal course. But adaptability is, after all, one of humanity's chief characteristics.

Other thinkers are more positive. Their optimism stems precisely from the present social and environmental crises. Can we really be so stupid as to continue to change the properties of the atmosphere, to degrade the natural world and to allow private companies to patent ingredients of food and medicine that have been used for millennia? Can we keep promoting an economic system which protects the interests of the rich while increasing numbers die of hunger? However, many politicians and mainline economists have accepted these bizarre and tragic consequences as inevitable aspects of the 'real world'.

It is only through an awareness of the direction in which we are heading that this outmoded mindset will change. The new thinking is now coming from organisations within the United Nations as well as from pressure groups, writers, scientists, economists and legislators who have minds that are open to new opportunities.

The reductionist approach to science, where each subject is studied in isolation, is now being challenged, too. Can scientists widen their imagination to encompass the interconnectedness of all life? New thinking asks us to respect the infinite diversity of nature and to work out how we can share the world without harm to its other creatures. The new thinking says that an economic system based on growth, though pleasant for some while it lasts, is ultimately doomed. We must now be masters of our technologies, using them to deliver benefits, not being seduced by them into unpredictable and dangerous experiments - as happened with nuclear power. The new thinking urges legislators to adopt the precautionary principle. It shows how we can achieve a stable and sustainable economy for all humanity. It shows that we can rediscover culture and deeper levels of personal and social fulfillment. It shows that human spirituality, human culture and our 'housekeeping', the economy, are deeply intertwined.

The new thinking reflects the Universal Declaration of Human Rights that 'all human beings are born free and equal in dignity and rights' – all, whether Swiss or Swazi, have equal rights to a clean planet that has a healthy future.

Don't curse the darkness, light a candle.

Cod

a symbol for our times

'After you, sir...'

The best fishing grounds in the world were off the coast of New England and the prize fish were cod. On Cabot's return from there in 1497 it was reported "the sea is swarming with fish which can be taken not only with the net but in baskets let down with a stone". A hundred years later cod were reported as big as a man and the fishing grounds served the whole of Europe.

Cod swim in large shoals just above the sea bed. They have a long life cycle, spawning only when, after four years, they are large enough. When trawl nets were introduced they scooped up all the fish, big and small, and few lasted long enough to spawn.

It was not until the 1980s that the coastal fishermen of New England realised that, thanks to big off-shore trawlers, the cod were disappearing, but the US government took no action. So by 1992 the cod were gone. With the fish went the fishermen. Their skills in navigation, gutting, net mending and fish marketing didn't help them. They were also a unique species that will be hard to replace. The tourists who come to enjoy the picturesque sailing ships in Gloucester harbour are now served filleted cod from Russia and fishermen cut the hotel lawns.

Fishermen will now have to wait up to fifteen years for the stocks of cod to return, if they ever do. Young cod are no longer migrating to warmer waters to spawn, perhaps because there are no older cod to lead them. Arctic cod, which have no market value, are moving in and they eat Atlantic-cod eggs and larvae. Other species and other predators are upsetting the natural balance and may also prevent rejuvenation of the cod stocks. So the most prolific fishing grounds in the world may now be dead.

It is a different story in Norway where there was also a crisis in the 1980s. Fish stocks were seriously depleted and catches were falling. The government took drastic action which put many fishermen and boat builders out of work, but within three years the stocks were improving and the fishing trade was saved.

Sixty percent of the world's ocean fisheries are now at or near the point at which yields decline, yet governments still provide massive subsidies to their fishing fleets. An international quota system has been introduced but even that has perverse effects: a third of the fish caught are simply thrown back dead, and only the higher value catch retained for the quota.

Cod caught in the North Sea per hour

1995   1996   1997

30 Cod

FACT The world's fishing industry produces $70 billion worth of fish. It receives $54 billion in subsidies.

But the story gets worse. Warmer water is depleting some species. Chemicals from rivers cause plankton blooms which deprive fish of oxygen. Fish farming is a partial solution and is on the increase, but it has severe problems too: interbreeding passes defective genes to wild fish, the farms act as hothouses for disease, and intensively used antibiotics and pesticides pollute coastal waters. The farms also need a lot of fish-food - it takes five kilogrammess of trawled wild fish (yes, it's made into fish food) from countries like Peru to feed one kilogramme of farmed Atlantic salmon. Thus Peruvian coastal fishermen are deprived of their staple diet and of their livelihood – just to serve the sophisticated tastes of the rich.

Freshwater species have also declined globally. The 1995 catch was 45% lower than that of 1970. Shrimp farms in East Asia are rarely productive for more than five to ten years, after which the land is unusable due to severe pollution; this temporary industry produces cheap shrimps and undercuts the sustainable production of traditional shrimp farmers.

There will only be hope if destructive practices are outlawed; if governments stop giving tens of billions of dollars in subsidies for overfishing; if the certification of seafood from well-managed sources is promoted; and if designated no-fishing zones are introduced.

Cod have been called 'the fish that changed the world'. They are now a warning to the world.

STOP PRESS! Cod are now on the Endangered Species list.

Cod
Mark Kurlansky
Vintage 1999
ISBN 0 099268 70 1

Don't Predict!

just be systematic

"Heavier-than-air flying machines are impossible" declared the eminent physicist Lord Kelvin in 1895. The chairman of IBM was wrong, too: "I think there is a world market for maybe five computers" said Thomas Watson in 1943. Then scientists predicted that 'nuclear' electricity would be too cheap to meter, and that oil would become scarce by the 1990s; we now extract more than ever. Anyway, we like to think that something will replace oil if it does run out, so why not carry on using it as before? Predictions and their failures can both be misleading.

Instead of guessing at the future we should think systematically about the past and the present - about things we actually know - and we must live within the rules set by nature. In a world of finite resource, what is used today will be denied our children - that simple logic avoids the uncertainty of when it might run out. There are four principles of sustainability that need to be respected, systematically:

♦ All the toxic minerals like mercury, or fossil resources which we dig out of the earth, refine, and use, will eventually degrade back into the land, water and air and cause cumulative pollution. *We must not extract more than can be safely contained or re-absorbed.*

♠ We live in a balanced ecology that evolved over a period of four billion years. When we introduce new, stable and persistent molecules, plants or creatures which are alien to this balance, they will cause problems somewhere, somehow. *We must not allow these products of society to increase in nature.*

♣ The world's flora, moisture and biodiversity form interconnected natural cycles that support life and a stable atmosphere. *We must not diminish this life-support system.*

♥ The fourth principle concerns equity. The poor, i.e. 80% of the world population who do not share our prosperity, will not sign up to any agreement that is manifestly unfair. *We must recognise that all people in the world need the benefits of nature - equally.*

We must test each human activity systematically and reject it if it offends any of the above principles. There is nothing woolly about sustainability; it is hard-edged, uncompromising, quantifiable and scientifically rigorous. The rules are set by nature, not by man.

The financial world is similar. Over the last couple of years commentators from time to time predicted that the American Dow Jones Index was about to tumble, yet it has steadily risen beyond all expectation; but, in the future - who knows?

Predictions can be self-fulfilling. The very act of participating in markets influences those markets. The world hangs on the words of Alan Greenspan, chairman of the Federal Reserve. If he wanted he could bring the whole pack of cards tumbling down by making a rash prediction; no wonder his face is so heavily lined. Yet he prefers to remain inscrutable - "if I seem unduly clear to you" he once told a congressman "you must have misunderstood what I said".

Every businessman and gambler would love to predict the future accurately, and every day the financial pages try to help them. But the most superficial look at the financial system indicates that it is inherently unjust, unstable and as predictable as the weather. And we leave it to the experts who have a vested interest in keeping it inscrutable. The best we can do is keep our fingers crossed in the hope that we may strike lucky.

The economy, like our environmental intervention, has grown exponentially and no one can predict where this will lead. But it should be obvious that we will be in deep trouble if we cannot re-model it to protect the ecosystem and to move, systematically, towards equity and stability.

Playing Safe
Jonathon Porritt
Thames and Hudson 2000
ISBN 0 500 28073 8

Ozone Layer

a ray of hope

If there were no ozone in the stratosphere there would be little life on earth.

Ozone is a gas, a form of oxygen. It is dispersed within a twenty-mile layer of the upper atmosphere where it shields us from ultraviolet (UV) radiation. It is so dilute that, if it were all brought down to sea level, it would be no thicker than a china plate.

In the 1970s scientists worried that within fifty years the ozone layer might reduce by 3%. By the late 1980s this had already happened! But, even worse, by 1996 a 'hole' 3 times the size of the U.S.A. had developed over the Antarctic, a hole was growing over the Arctic, and there was a 20% reduction over much of the world.

UV-B has had a lot of publicity because it causes skin cancers. But it also reduces resistance to AIDS, tuberculosis and herpes; causes cataracts and blindness; kills plankton in the sea, thus affecting the fish population and also reducing plankton's pivotal role in extracting carbon dioxide from the air - which plankton does more effectively than trees. It reduces the growth and yield of most food crops. With increased exposure to UV-B the genes in some plants jump from one site to another in the genome, causing mutations and disrupting the plant's development and fertility. Changes to the DNA of plants and animals could permeate the food chain.

How is the ozone layer destroyed?

The major culprits are chlorofluoro-carbon (CFCs), though halid-containing substances, widely used in pesticides, are partly responsible. CFCs are artificial chemicals which have been widely used in propellants, refrigerants, insulation, cleaning agents and packaging. They are non-toxic, have no smell and are non-flammable, so, for forty years they were considered benign: there seemed no reason to restrict their use. But they offend a fundamental law of sustainability being stable gases not found in nature, and somewhere, somehow, they were bound to cause problems. We can now only regret that legislators did not invoke the precautionary principle earlier.

FACT When CFC molecules are exposed to strong UV radiation in the upper atmosphere they are broken up and release chlorine atoms, which attack the ozone. **A single chlorine atom can destroy many thousands of ozone molecules.** If CFC emissions were stopped today the chemical reactions would continue for decades.

Other processes contribute to ozone damage: the destruction of tropical forests; increases in cattle ranching; cattle-feed with a high protein content; artificial fertilisation of rice; the use of chemicals like the methyl bromide in pesticides. It is not a simple matter of cause and effect; there are many interconnections.

There are, however, signs of hope. In 1987, the 'Montreal Protocol' required industrial countries to halt CFC production and it banned trading in products containing CFCs. It was based on the 'precautionary principle' before scientists actually agreed that there was a problem. The conference also set up a fund to help countries change. Although the protocol calls for a global ban by 2006 many industries, particularly in the USA, have acted early. But there are still problems: Russia's economic crisis has slowed its programme and a black-market in CFCs has developed. A refrigerator in every home in China will massively increase its use of CFCs, and the World Trade Organization could decide that any restrictions infringe free trade rules. But if all goes well the ozone layer might be back to normal in fifty years.

State of the World 2000
Worldwatch Institute
Earthscan 2000
ISBN 1 85383 680 X

Carbon and Temperature

uncharted territory

The earth's temperature fluctuates, but it has been remarkably stable during human history.

The temperature at any particular location is affected by many things. Our distance from the sun varies on a 100,000 year cycle, the earth 'tilts' over a period of 40,000 years and it 'wobbles' over a period of 23,000 years. These periods are so long that they are of only academic interest for our present concerns. The sun's intensity, too, varies. The earth reflects heat depending on the amount of snow (white) or vegetation (dark), and this can accentuate temperature change. (When snow or polar ice melts, more solar heat is absorbed by the dark ground, causing increased temperatures and faster melting - a positive feedback effect).

During human history the global temperature has been regulated primarily by concentrations of greenhouse gases in the atmosphere, particularly carbon dioxide. Air bubbles, trapped at the poles, provide an accurate record of their concentrations. These show a low content of carbon dioxide during the Ice Ages, below 240 ppmv (parts per million by volume), with higher concentrations during interglacial periods, but never rising above 300 ppmv. Our present interglacial period started 10,000 years ago when concentrations rose to a narrow band between 260 and 280 ppmv. This provided stable conditions that allowed humans to practice settled agriculture and develop civilizations. Concentrations started to rise above this narrow

Take time to look at this graph; it is fascinating.

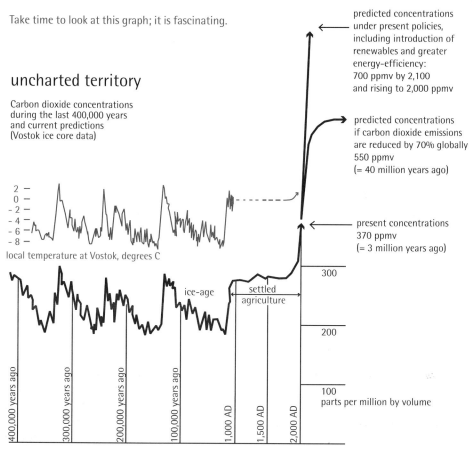

uncharted territory

Carbon dioxide concentrations
during the last 400,000 years
and current predictions
(Vostok ice core data)

predicted concentrations
under present policies,
including introduction of
renewables and greater
energy-efficiency:
700 ppmv by 2,100
and rising to 2,000 ppmv

predicted concentrations
if carbon dioxide emissions
are reduced by 70% globally
550 ppmv
(= 40 million years ago)

present concentrations
370 ppmv
(= 3 million years ago)

local temperature at Vostok, degrees C

ice-age

settled
agriculture

300

200

100
parts per million by volume

400,000 years ago
300,000 years ago
200,000 years ago
100,000 years ago
1,000 AD
1,500 AD
2,000 AD

band with the Industrial Revolution. Early this century they exceeded the highest levels ever experienced in the 400,000 years for which measurements are available. Recently concentrations have been increasing at a totally unprecedented rate, now passing 370 ppmv, way above anything ever experienced before. Even if fundamental measures are now taken, they will continue to rise to at least 450ppmv.

In order to advise the Rio Summit in 1992, the Intergovernmental Panel on Climate Change (IPCC) tried to predict how high temperatures might rise during the coming century, and their 'best guess' was 3°C above pre-industrial levels.

However, a poll of the IPCC scientists found that 51 out of 113 believed that 'runaway' global warming was a possibility. Fifteen of them believed it 'probable'. In the decade since the IPCC made these predictions, mean global temperatures have been rising faster than predicted in the IPCC's 'worst case' scenario. We are in uncharted territory. Global warming, due to increased carbon concentrations, may have gone beyond the point of no return.

Professor William Nordhaus of Yale University, Nobel Prize winner for economics, calculated that the US could afford to spend no more than 2% of GDP to combat global warming, because that was the value of the agriculture and forestry sectors which would be affected by climate change. His calculation formed the basis of US negotiations at Rio World Summit (though, in fact, the US spends nothing like this figure). He ignored the fact that people cannot survive without food, so the monetary value of agriculture would greatly increase if it were seriously harmed by changed climatic conditions and food became scarce. This would be amusing if it did not demonstrate the quality of economic advice on which great nations take decisions.

STOP PRESS! *"Levels of CO_2 are now well on the way to those found in the Eocene period when the World was ice-free and England was a steaming mangrove forest".*
New Scientist 26.8.2000

FACT CO_2 emissions show a 99.5% correlation with World Industrial Product (WIP) over the last 100 years. 95% of the energy used by humankind is obtained by burning fossil fuels. Investment in solar and wind energy may allow more economic activity with less pollution, but this does not yet show in global figures. So, as prosperity and consumption have increased, so have greenhouse gas emissions.

FACT Referring to anticipated climate change the Royal Commission on Environmental Pollution says: "this combination of magnitude and rate of change would exceed anything that species and ecosystems have experienced in the last half million years."

FACT The UK export credit department is supporting coal-fired power plants in China and India, ensuring that these nations will become permanently dependent on fossil fuels.

FACT Carbon Tax:

CO_2 is emitted in a million different ways but enters the economy from less than a dozen sources. Carbon Tax should therefore replace the Energy Tax and be levied at the point of entry where it is easy to collect, impossible to evade, and where it does not distort the economy. Carbon tax should be the major source of income for the government, reducing income tax and contributing towards a Citizen's Income. Fossil-fuel prices will, of course, rise and special measures will need to be introduced to prevent fuel-poverty.

If there is more greenhouse gas up there than ever before, are you sure that we can go on adding to it?

God's Last Offer
Ed Ayres
Four Walls Eight Windows. 1999
ISBN 1 56858 125 4

Global Warming

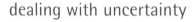

dealing with uncertainty

Two hundred million years ago forests covered the land, the atmosphere had a high content of carbon dioxide, the air was 10°C warmer and the oceans were 70 metres higher. Gradually, photosynthesis and phytoplankton captured carbon from the air and laid it down in the crust of the earth. The concentration of greenhouse gases reduced, and water levels fell. Greenhouse gases make the earth habitable; without them we would be 30°C colder, frozen and lifeless. For the last 10,000 years there has been remarkable climate stability with average global temperatures around 15°C. This stability made it possible for humans to cultivate land, to settle, and to develop civilizations.

Discovery of fossil fuels about 250 years ago started the industrial revolution. By digging up and burning this fossil resource we have been releasing carbon back into the atmosphere where, with other 'greenhouse gases', it blankets the earth preventing solar heat from radiating back into space. This is the main cause of human-enhanced global warming.

The influence on climate of the various gases in the atmosphere was first identified in 1827 by Joseph Fourier, a French mathematician. John Tyndall, an Irish scientist, took on the idea. Then in 1898 Arrhenius, a Swedish scientist, coined the phrase 'greenhouse effect' and predicted that, if concentrations of carbon dioxide in the atmosphere doubled, the global climate would warm by 4-6°C, figures remarkably close to current predictions. Scientists continued to argue for a hundred more years but the connection between greenhouse gases and climate is now universally accepted.

Human-induced warming may set off non-human natural processes that cause additional warming which may run out of control. These are called positive feedback effects. A serious concern is the methane trapped under the arctic icecap and in tundra; methane is twenty times more effective than CO_2 as a greenhouse gas, and could cause irreversible runaway warming if these massive reservoirs are released. The British Met Office is also concerned that atmospheric changes will cause a die-back of forests which will in turn reduce CO_2 absorption and further accelerate the warming process. The Royal Commission's July 2000 report, mentioned below, sets out the situation with clarity and should be required reading for all decision-makers.

The first world-ecosystem to suffer critically is that of the coral reefs around the world. Corals have been likened to the miner's canary - if the canary tips off its perch the miner knows he is in serious trouble.

The 'best-guess' scenario has sea levels rising by about 50cm due purely to the expansion (from warming) of water. Sea levels will rise more if glaciers continue to melt. If Antarctic land-based icecaps are dislodged (some of them are over three miles thick) the increase in sea levels will be dramatic, and London would be among the first cities to be flooded.

As nuclear power does not release greenhouse gases we can expect political pressure to ignore its very real dangers. To avoid this we must obtain all our energy from renewable sources, leaving fossil resources for more valuable purposes.

FACT Energy, dams, traffic, aeroplanes and agriculture, all of which pollute, attract subsidies of $900 billion a year worldwide. In the words of the Earth Council: "the world is spending hundreds of billions of dollars annually to subsidise its own destruction".

There are some slight movements which indicate that the new energy revolution has started: Denmark plans to get half its energy from off-shore wind farms. The US has a 'million solar roofs' programme. BP Petroleum is investing massively in solar energy. Some developers are realising that solar collecting façades are cheaper than covering their prestige buildings in marble. In Britain, new Peabody Estates will get all their electricity from solar collectors. Sadly Britain lags behind the market leaders in these new technologies.

Decisions made only on the basis of current prices are stupid and short-sighted. The price of renewable energy sources is at present higher than fossil fuel technology, but falling fast. If reduced concentrations of carbon dioxide in the atmosphere reduce global warming and save London from flooding, the marginal extra cost will be seen as an investment of superlative value. When legislators eventually realise that fossil fuel is causing immense damage they will take measures to prevent people from using it. The cost of continuing to use coal, oil and gas will then become prohibitive. The far-sighted will see this shift in energy use as the biggest business opportunity for two hundred years. Companies, architects, engineers and builders that embrace renewable technology now will have a future. Those that are wedded to an outdated technology will fade away.

Photovoltaic cells capture energy from the sun and convert it into electricity. There is enough solar energy hitting our buildings for all our energy needs - even in the UK, even in winter. Fuel cell technology converts and stores this for use at any time of day or night, and the only 'waste' product is drinking water. This technology needs no fuel other than solar radiation and can serve individual buildings; it does not need an electricity grid. No wonder the oil companies and public utilities have suggested that renewable energy can not meet our needs; it will put them out of business.

A solar revolution is in progress. A revolution far greater even than the Industrial Revolution.

If half a degree of global warming is causing hurricanes, cyclones and floods, what will three degrees do?

FACT Holders of £9 billion worth of BP Amoco shares voted against oil extraction in the Arctic. The directors ignored them and are proceeding with the Northstar project.

FACT 1998 was the hottest year on record. Flooding of the Yangtze river displaced 56 million people. 26 million were made homeless in Bangladesh. Hurricane Mitch killed 18,000 people.

FACT The collapse of the West Antarctic ice sheet would raise ocean levels by 6 metres. The Royal Commission on Environmental Pollution says: "The balance of opinion appears to be against this happening, but it remains a possibility."

FACT On present trends, damage to property will exceed the Gross World Product (GWP) within two generations. The insurance industry now supports measures to reduce climate change.

Energy - The Changing Climate
Royal Commission on Environmental Pollution
HMSO. 2000
ISBN 0 10 147492 X

Europe Cooling

ocean currents

For us in Britain a warmer climate sounds rather pleasant. But once climate change seriously affects Britain we may take a different view. Ironically, many scientists now fear that global warming may cause the regional cooling of Europe.

Most scare stories relate to other parts of the world. The Met Office has predicted that eighty million people in Asia could be flooded due to climate instability which we, the industrialised countries, are causing. Since their report, disasters in Bangladesh, Orissa and Mozambique have demonstrated the human suffering that this will entail. Some island states may simply disappear due to a rise in sea levels. But some disasters are getting closer to home: 300 million trees in France have been felled by a hurricane, and the dykes of Holland are threatened by rising sea levels. It is ocean currents that might harm us.

Ocean currents have a critical impact on climate. The deep water of the 'conveyor belt' in the Atlantic Ocean, which drives the Gulf Stream, takes about a thousand years to circulate at low level from the Arctic to the Antarctic, so it was assumed that these currents provided long-term stability. But recently this assumption has been put in doubt. The first shock came when currents in the Mediterranean went into reverse in just one year. Then the deep sea current between Greenland and Norway did the same. 100,000 years ago, average temperatures in Greenland moved up and down by as much as 7°C in a decade, probably due to the switching on and off of Atlantic ocean currents. Although average world temperatures have only risen 0.6°C in recent years, some arctic weather stations now show warming of 5°C. The thickness of some ice sheets has halved and their area has reduced by sixteen percent.

When ice forms from seawater it leaves the salt behind. The resulting heavy salty water drops to the ocean floor, creating the 'pumps' that drive the Gulf Stream. The water in these pumps is now getting less saline, because less water is freezing, it is being joined by fresh water from melting icebergs, and it is getting warmer. If this process continues, a critical point will be reached and the pumps will stop. The Gulf Stream brings warmth from the tropics to Britain, and without it our climate would resemble that of Labrador or parts of Siberia and our agriculture would be destroyed. We would then have a crisis as serious as that currently being faced by many Pacific islands.

Climate and ocean currents are still little understood. We may not be able to predict the precise outcome of an increase in greenhouse gases, but the range of options is fairly well understood. Military planners always look at the

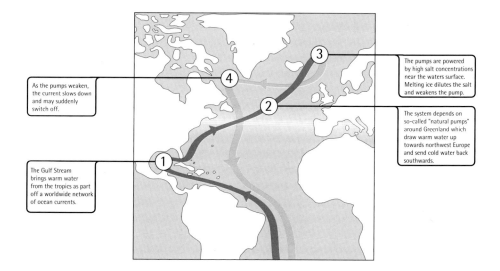

As the pumps weaken, the current slows down and may suddenly switch off.

The pumps are powered by high salt concentrations near the waters surface. Melting ice dilutes the salt and weakens the pump.

The system depends on so-called "natural pumps" around Greenland which draw warm water up towards northwest Europe and send cold water back southwards.

The Gulf Stream brings warm water from the tropics as part off a worldwide network of ocean currents.

worst-case scenario and ensure that this is covered. Strangely, the opposite is done with climate: the Intergovernmental Panel on Climate Change only included the 'best guess' scenario in its 1990 report in order to avoid sensationalist reports in the media! Worst-case scenarios have to be proved before we take action. By then it may be too late.

If we wish to keep our green and pleasant land we, and the world at large, must take systematic action to stop adding greenhouse gases to the atmosphere. This policy is still resisted by oil, gas and coal interests, and by the World Bank which during the 1990s subsidised fossil-energy seven times as much as renewable-energy projects.

One can't repeat too often that adequate technologies already exist for generating almost all our energy needs from renewable resources. So why don't we? The answer to that may be in our economic system. It locks us into a mindset that may prove to be suicidal.

FACT The Royal Commission on Environmental Pollution confirms: "Some models predict that the North Atlantic ocean circulation system, which transports heat from the sub-tropics towards Europe, might shut down."

Water

fresh water is running out

Rain is our only sustainable source of fresh water. We ignore this simple fact at our peril.

Fly over the prairie states of America and you will see clusters of dark circles, like tiny coins, in a desert landscape. Actually, each circle is cultivation, half a mile in diameter, irrigated from a single drop-well and rotating arm. Previously the land had thin grass and wandering herds of buffalo. Now it produces wheat with a higher yield than anywhere in the world. The grain exports from this area are vital for financing America's imports and are a major contributor to feeding the growing world population. It is a miracle of modern agriculture.

Underneath lies the biggest aquifer in the world. Water from melting glaciers seeped into gravel at the end of the last ice age and has been there ever since. It was found in the 1920s and its extraction really got under way in the 1960s. Four to six feet of water is now extracted each year and nature puts back only half an inch. It could last five years, it could last thirty years; no one knows. Farmers believed that this breadbasket was so valuable that the government would provide a massive water project to meet their needs if it ever ran out, like diverting the Mississippi. So they did nothing to economise on the use of water. The future is more likely to be a return of the Dust Bowl that devastated the area in the 1930s.

San Francisco

Denver

Los Angeles

El Paso

Dallas

Detroit

New York

Washington

Most freshwater in the world is in aquifers, and a quarter of the world's people depend on them for drinking. Yet all over the world the aquifers are being depleted. Some are finite reservoirs which will never be replaced. Some are replenished from surface water. But even these have problems: sixty percent of the nitrate fertiliser we apply when farming remains in the soil and gradually seeps into the groundwater where it is joined by such pollutants as sewage from leaking pipes and petro-chemicals from rusty fuel tanks. Already a major aquifer in China has serious problems with nitrate contamination, and some in Britain are laced with benzene.

Irrigation requires organisation, so brought the first civilizations into existence. But salt may have destroyed them.

With irrigation, if there is an impervious substrate the water does not drain; salts are drawn to the roots of plants. If the land is drained the salt accumulates in rivers, and evaporation from dam reservoirs concentrates the saltiness. By 1973 the salinity of the Colorado River, where it crossed the border into Mexico's most fertile region, was liquid death to plants.

Water is more valuable than gold - you can't drink gold. We are as dependent on water to drink as we are on air to breathe. But we know even less about groundwater than we know about the weather. How much pollution is already in the ground? How long will it take to get into aquifers? How fast will it spread? How can we extract the pollution? The cost of purifying water is escalating, though this is not charged to the polluters – the farmers, the oil companies and the sewerage system. 'Let them drink bottled water' will be the cry when it becomes too expensive to provide clean tap water. But how long will the bottles last?

Dams are the other source of irrigation. It is strange that the US followed the communist policy of providing virtually free water to its farmers from federal-funded dams, thus encouraging waste on a grand scale - just as in Russia. There was an orgy of construction before dam-building finally stopped in the early 1980s. Virtually all US rivers now have dams. There are 80,000: 50,000 of them significant, 2,000 of them among the biggest construction projects in the world. But the dams have a finite life as they gradually fill with silt.

The US is now casting envious eyes on Canada's abundant free-flowing rivers and, when the US gets desperate, its neighbours have much to fear. Do the Canadians want to lose their beautiful valleys, their salmon and their white-water rafting?

FACT Global consumption of freshwater is doubling every twenty years. At present:
- 10% is used by people
- 65% is used by industrial agriculture
- 25% is used by industry.

FACT One billion people already suffer from a shortage of fresh water. It is estimated that two-thirds of the world population will suffer severe water shortages in 25 years. This shortage is entirely man-made - we could choose to give priority to people rather than to industry or to industrial agriculture.

FACT The World Bank is withholding support from India unless it makes progress in privatising water. Tribals can no longer draw water from an ancient tank in Maharashtra because it is now exclusively used by Coca Cola, who can pay more.

FACT Export Credit Agencies (ECAs): The Three Gorges Dam in China will forcibly displace two million people and inundate vast areas of arable land. It is expected to silt up within fifty years, making it useless for irrigation or power generation, and putting it at risk of catastrophic collapse in a heavy flood. It is made possible by Western ECAs, with no public consultation, as a means of securing lucrative contracts for their national companies. The funding of major projects through ECAs, which receive their money from tax payers, is a major source of Third World Debt.

FACT In 2,400 BC, irrigated fields in Sumeria produced 2,500 litres of barley per hectare, a respectable yield even by modern standards. By 1,700 BC the yield fell to 900 litres per hectare. Soon afterwards, crop failures began - and that was the end of Sumeria. Most of the great civilizations that depended on irrigation went the same way: salts came to the surface and destroyed their agriculture.

But Egypt, fertile since the Pharaohs, was an exception. Each year the Nile floods the fields, deposits rich new silt and flushes the surface salts out to sea. Well, it did until 1970 when the Aswan high dam was built. The silt no longer renews the land each year, salts are no longer washed way, bilharzia is rampant, and the delta fishery is declining fast. What's more, the reservoir behind the dam is rapidly filling with the silt that should be fertilizing the fields below.

Cadillac Desert
Mark Reisner
Penguin Books 1993
ISBN 0 14 01 7824 4

Ecological Footprints

the rich wear big boots

Kerala is beautiful. Canals shaded by coconut palms, markets beside the water, kids playing on the banks. Walk the streets of Kovalum and you catch laughing eyes as groups chat and women display their colourful saris. There are plenty of festivals. Then return to Europe and you are struck by how drab and glum everyone looks.

Kerala is one of the poorest states in India. Yet the infant mortality rate in Kerala is lower than in some European countries; life expectancy is 72 years (higher than that of black people in the US); 95 percent of Keralans over the age of seven can read and write; it has a higher proportion of its population with postgraduate degrees than the US. Importantly, population is stable or falling. It is a matriarchal society but the low birth rate is due to the high level of female literacy (the only exception is the Moslem community, because of the low status of their women).

What has all this to do with 'ecological footprints'? An 'ecological footprint' is the productive land necessary to support people in their lifestyle. An American or European gets his food, minerals and oil from all over the world and all these things use some of the world's limited productive land. His 'footprint' is larger than an Indian's. The world has only 1.5 hectares available for each person. But, to support its present patterns of consumption, the world needs 2.3 hectares of productive land per person. This excessive footprint is trampling the world's available resources, for example:

7.5% of all arable land is abandoned every decade;

- the Earth's forest, freshwater and marine environments have reduced by 30% in thirty years;
- a third of all fish species and a quarter of all mammal species are in danger of extinction.

So while the population is increasing, the world's resource base is decreasing at an alarming rate. If everyone adopted the Western lifestyle we would need five earths to support us! So we either multiply the area of the earth by five, or match our lifestyle to the earth's available natural wealth. The latter is rather easier .

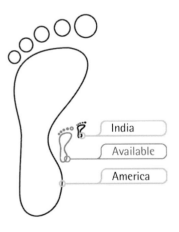

India

Available

America

Back to Kerala: they are not harming the earth; their education, health and longevity are comparable with the West's; their women have equality; their population is stable. They show that one can have a satisfactory lifestyle with a footprint that is well within the carrying capacity of the world – *i.e. sustainable*. Perhaps we should be looking at their culture for lessons in how to create a sustainable culture for ourselves.

FACT When Gandhi was asked for his views on Western civilization he replied: "I think it would be a good idea".

FACT The US, pioneer of industrial agriculture, has lost half its topsoil in the last century.

FACT The 20% of people living in the rich countries consume 86% of the world's resources.

Creating Sustainable Cities
Herbert Girardet
Schumacher Briefing
Green Books 1999
ISBN 1 870098 77 3

Inequality

a bequest of the 20th century

In spite of all the talk about economic growth, development and aid, inequality is growing at an accelerating rate.

During the last century the industrialised world gained unimaginable wealth while many other nations moved into abject poverty. We have emerged from that century thinking that this is natural and inevitable. Four-fifths of the world's population has to make do with only 14% of the world's wealth; the rest goes to support the living standards of the rich minority.

In spite of the development of agriculture, scientific knowledge and modern technology, the wealth of the poorest group has actually fallen. The wealth of the 225 richest people in the world has nearly tripled in the last six years and their assets now equal the entire annual income of half the world's population.

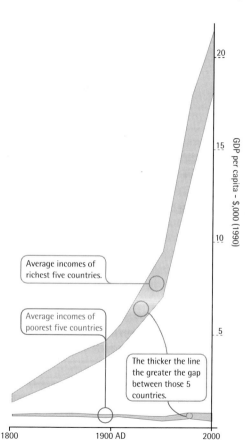

GDP per capita - $,000 (1990)

Average incomes of richest five countries.

Average incomes of poorest five countries

The thicker the line the greater the gap between those 5 countries.

1800   1900 AD   2000

FACT The income gap between the top and bottom fifth of the world's people jumped from 30:1 in 1960 to 74:1 in 1997.

FACT The 20% of world population in rich countries have 80% of the world's GDP.

FACT In 1976 Switzerland was 50 times richer than Mozambique. In 1997 it was 500 times richer.

FACT The top 1% of households in the US have more wealth than the entire bottom 95%.

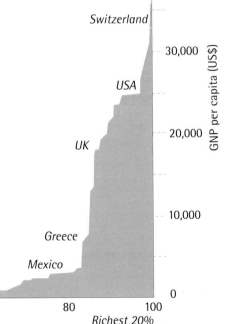

Distribution of the world's wealth

A similar trend is at work within Britain. In 1980 one in ten of the UK population earned less than half the current average income; now one in four suffer this definition of poverty, and one in five of our children live below the official poverty line. But the financial sector still awards itself million-pound bonuses.

We are constantly told that the way to reduce poverty is through economic growth. Experience tells us that this is not true. The Human Poverty Index 1998 (HPI-2) for industrial countries, prepared by the United Nations, showed that Sweden, with one of the lowest rates of economic growth per person, had the best record of human welfare. Whereas the United States, with the highest rate of economic growth (and a higher per capita GDP than Sweden), had more people who were 'functionally illiterate' (20.7%) than the proportion in any other industrialised country; the highest proportion of population below the income poverty line (19.1%); and the greatest number of people who did not expect to reach the age of sixty (13%). Ten percent of the US population depended on private charity for food.

There must be something structurally wrong with a world economic system that allows these inequalities to grow. Yet economists still believe that further economic growth will relieve poverty. And politicians believe that new initiatives on debt, aid and global trade can buck the imperatives of an economic system which, by its fundamental laws, transfers wealth from the poor to the rich.

FACT A major cause of inequality is an economy based on charging interest. Money flows from the poor who need to borrow, to the rich who have spare cash to lend.

FACT A recent poll found that 77% of Americans believe their government has no responsibility to "take care of the very poor people who can't take care of themselves."

Sharing the World
Carley and Spapens
Earthscan 1998
ISBN 1 85383 463 7

Weapons of War

an environmental issue

'Nine out of ten Americans exterminated'. This would be a dramatic headline if any television or newspaper survived to carry it or any viewer had eyes to read it. But it actually happened in the 16th century.

In 1527 a hundred-and-seventy Spaniards in search of gold walked into an army of a hundred thousand Inca; Pizarro captured Atahuallpa, the Inca were routed and piles of gold were transferred to Europe. Although the Spaniards' initial success was due to sharp steel weapons, horses, helmets, body armour and deception, the extermination that followed was due to germs. Native Americans had no immunity to European diseases like smallpox. Novel weapons and alien germs changed the course of history.

In the last century nuclear weapons created new tensions. The policy of mutually-assured-destruction was, of course, MAD and could have finished us all off. Luckily, it didn't. But the threat remains. Nuclear capacity confers great power status, as India has found. Nations with nuclear weapons continue to proliferate, the US still refuses to sign the Comprehensive Test Ban Treaty or the Chemical Weapons Convention, and it still wants to take 'defence' into space.

In this new century we have new causes for conflict, new targets and new weapons:

● Conflict is being *caused* by environmental degradation and inequality - water scarcity, flooding, desertification, disparity of wealth and destitution. The number of regional wars is increasing. All except one of the 40 wars fought in the 1990s were civil or guerrilla conflicts within national boundaries.

● It has become more difficult to locate *targets*. When there is a national figurehead like Saddam Hussein, Nato can lob bombs into his country from a safe distance, and bring it to its knees by causing starvation and disease through sanctions. But it is more difficult to find and bomb an individual terrorist like Osama bin Laden.

● The weapons are new. Poor states can now get access to missiles carrying radioactive waste. Non-state groups can obtain chemicals, for example the nerve-gas Sarin used by a Tokyo cult to kill commuters. Computer viruses can be sent over the ether. The ultimate horror would be for small groups to use biological agents, since viruses or bacteria, once released, can spread of their own accord. There are already stocks around the world and in the US it is not illegal to own biological weapons like anthrax; recipes for them are on the internet.

The majority-nations, once colonies, then became young-nations-with-a-bright-future. But now the wealthy minority glowers at what it sees as a risk-prone zone, a breeding ground for crisis, suffering from epidemics, violence, desertification, over-population and corruption.

However these majority-nations of the South hold the raw materials, the genetic richness, and the potential markets that the minority-nations covet, and which they aim to plunder.

Hope can only come when security is no longer achieved through military force in a world linked by communications but divided by desperation and massive disparity in wealth. Our security is inseparably linked to a healthy environment and equity for the diverse cultures of the world.

Guns, Germs and Steel
Jared Diamond
Mackays 1997
ISBN 0 224 03809 5

An Oxymoron?

sustainable development

In Bali fruit fell from trees and life revolved around music and festival. In Ladakh culture flourished in an extreme climate. In Kenya the Maasai lived in harmony with migrating herds, probably showing continuity from the very origin of our species - Abel, beloved of God, till slain by Cain, the modern farmer and park ranger. China discovered most of our inventions and decided not to use them. In ancient Greece anyone who did not spend much of his time in public debate was dismissed as an 'idiot'. Islam showed how a classless society was possible, developed philosophy and built the most engagingly beautiful buildings like the Taj and the Alhambra. Cultures grew in response to regional conditions, and excess time and wealth were used for buildings, art, ceremonies and jewellery. For four thousand years of civilization consumption hardly increased but we are left with evidence of wonderful cultural richness.

Then on 20 January 1949, in his inauguration speech, President Truman defined most of the world as "underdeveloped areas" where "greater production is the key to prosperity and peace". Set against this was Gandhi's previous warning in 1908 "should India ever resolve to imitate England" he said "it would be the ruin of the nation". Gandhi lost and Truman won.

The majority-nations took up the idea of 'development' with enthusiasm. Rich countries cut slices from their cake-of-wealth to feed the poor, but they still believed that the magic cake would grow forever, and the rich would never need to reduce its portion. In the end everyone would be satisfied.

Within a few years it became apparent that development was not producing jobs, so 'manpower development' became the theme.

Then after ten years it was realised that hardship persisted so 'social development' was the key phrase at conferences, followed by the 'basic needs approach' and 'equitable development'. The one thing that could never be questioned was the concept of development itself.

Eventually it was realised that the magic cake was not growing and might even be shrinking. So 'sustainable development' was introduced. There is now an army of ecocrats drawing up papers and attending conferences, busily working out how to do more with less. Light bulbs become more efficient. Cars are shared and oil companies plant trees to absorb their fumes. Cities must be sustainable. The ecocrats struggle to bring appropriate technology, 'forgiveness' and justice to the poor. Even nature itself has been renamed 'natural capital' so that it can be included in the sums. It is all very comforting.

The driving force behind super-efficient 'sustainable' development is the 'no pain' theory, the promise of achieving justice in the world without having to redistribute our excessive wealth - or is it just putting off the unpalatable moment of truth when we realise that the cake is smaller than we thought and that it must be shared?

"Perhaps four thousand years of culture were rather more nourishing than fifty years of development."

FACT Development can be wiped out by human-induced global warming. Following Hurricane Mitch the Honduran president commented: "We lost in 72 hours what we have taken more than 50 years to build".

Planet Dialectics
Wolfgang Sachs
Zed Books 1999
ISBN 1 85649 701 1

Rio and Kyoto

slow progress

Putting it crudely, if we wish to save life on this earth as we know it, global carbon dioxide emissions must be cut by 60% - 80% of current levels. To achieve this we will have to reduce the use of fossil fuels drastically. This was the conclusion of a1990 report prepared by scientists of the Intergovernmental Panel on Climate Change (IPCC).

However, due to intense pressure from oil interests, it was not until 1995 that the IPCC was able to issue the unanimous, if minimalist, statement that "the balance of evidence suggests a discernible human influence on climate". Ten years after the initial warning, the 'balance of evidence' suggests that there has been no discernible influence by international conferences and millions of bureaucratic hours on the level of human-caused greenhouse gas emissions. During the last decade of the 20th century the climate followed the IPCC's worst-case scenario, not their mid-range forecast. The flooding of Mozambique is just one example of what is in store.

At the Earth Summit in Rio in 1992, Pacific Island states begged the industrialised nations, which have been responsible for global warming, to take effective action quickly. Rising sea levels will obliterate their countries.

But instead, the oil companies, usually in competition with each other, united to form the Global Climate Coalition (GCC). With massive funding they spread scientific doubt, disinformation and fear of financial decline; and their influence was so great that they did not just influence, they actually formed and coordinated American, Saudi and Kuwaiti policy at climate conferences. Their arguments, however puerile, are still eagerly championed by the American business community. (Some big players however, like Shell and BP, now admit that they were wrong.) In 1997, Friends of the Earth set up the 'Scorched Earth Award' for the worst 'carbon criminals'; the award was easily won by the GCC.

In 1997 at Kyoto a hundred countries, mainly of the North, agreed to reduce their greenhouse gas emissions to 5.2% below 1990 levels within fifteen years. So each country was given a quota based on its level of emissions. The more damage a country had caused in the past, the more it could pollute in the future – unfair, but at least it was an agreement. Even so the US Senate, influenced by the GCC, voted 95-0 not to ratify the treaty unless India also signed (India would have had a tiny quota because it emits so little). Nevertheless the Kyoto protocol was an historic first step.

Should we judge these world summits by intentions or by results? The average global temperature continues to rise faster than ever before in human history. We can expect catastrophic climate instability. Countries of the South face flooding, cyclones and desertification, with millions becoming environmental refugees. Pacific states face inundation (one group of islands has already been abandoned). Their sentiment was well expressed at Kyoto by the President of Nauru: "The willful destruction, with foreknowledge, of entire countries and cultures represents an unspeakable crime against humanity". If calamitous climate change occurs, as now seems distinctly possible, this inaction by the rich minority nations will overshadow all other acts of barbarism in the history of humankind.

FACT The US is threatening sanctions against the tiny Pacific republic of Nauru for being a tax haven. Meanwhile Nauru is in danger of being obliterated because of CO_2 emissions by the US and others.

The Carbon War
Jeremy Leggett
Allen Lane 1999
ISBN 0 71 399360 X

Trading Pollution Quotas

a practical approach

How can we eliminate pollution? The idea of 'trading' pollution quotas sounds bizarre, even vaguely immoral, but for developing countries, strangely enough, it might work. This is because the financial markets, whether we like it or not, are the most effective vehicles for controlling trade. Central control doesn't work; that is one thing the 20th century did prove. So how can the markets reduce pollution and help the poor?

The biggest threat the world has ever faced during human history is the rising level of greenhouse gases in the atmosphere. We must reduce emissions to a level that the world can sustain. There is no alternative. These gases are an essential part of a balanced ecosystem; it is only in excess that they become dangerous. But to get them back to a safe level, emissions will have to reduce by over 60%. Since financial markets are so powerful they should be designed to reward countries for reducing emissions. A mechanism for doing this is quite simple and obvious, and is only obscured by industrialised countries wriggling and squirming in their attempt to avoid paying a fair price for their resources. Here is how such a market could operate:

🌑 On average, everyone in the world is responsible for 4.21 tonnes of carbon dioxide emissions each year.

🌑 If the atmosphere can only sustain a limited quantity of carbon dioxide, should one person be allowed to emit a lot more than another?

Everyone should have an equal allowance, i.e. 4.21 tonnes at present but reducing with time.

An Indian 'emits' 0.81 tonnes on average and therefore has a surplus of 3.4 tonnes available for sale.

An average American 'emits' 19.53 tonnes. He therefore needs to buy 15.32 tonnes in order to maintain his lifestyle.

Multiplied by population this means that India has 3.2 billion tonnes of CO_2 for sale and the US needs to buy 4.1 billion tonnes. The US needs to buy the whole of India's surplus and more besides. Alternatively the US must reduce its emissions.

Trading on this basis means that money would flow from the rich nations, which are causing the climate havoc, to poor nations that are suffering it. The United Nations Development Programme commented: "Such flows would be neither aid nor charity. They would be the outcome of a free market mechanism that penalizes the richer nations' over-consumption of the global commons". Thus a fair market system for tradable quotas would result in a fairer world. Each nation's allowance could then gradually be reduced on an equal per capita basis to a globally sustainable level.

Not practical? Rich nations may not like the thought of inhabiting a fair and equitable world, but multinationals might not object - if a millionaire becomes a billionaire he is not going to drink any more Coca-Cola; but an Indian rising out of abject poverty becomes a marketing opportunity. But that's another story – and perhaps another clutch of problems.

What are the alternatives? Regions that suffer catastrophic loss due to pollution by the rich nations should have a case in international law; if so, their claim for damages would be considerably greater than the 'Third World Debt'. If neither equity nor legal redress can be obtained, they might resort to violence.

The Lugano Report
Susan George
Pluto 2000
ISBN 0 7453 1532 1

Domestic Tradable Quotas

towards equity in each country

It is, simply, grotesquely unfair that the rich get away with polluting the atmosphere on which the poor also rely. A method for reducing this unfairness, described in the previous chapter, could work locally, too. Everyone, however poor, would have something of value, either to use themselves, or to sell to others.

Diary Note:

> "It has been a good month - only took car out four times and walked into work every day - swipe-card used only half carbon quota - £450 credited to statement. Note in diary: protest to council; we must be the last city in the country still to run public services on the electricity grid! When will they connect to the off-shore wind farm and reduce our rates?"

In Britain, for example, under the Domestic Tradable Quota (DTQ) system you would receive a ration of carbon units each month. The amount of carbon fuel (e.g. petrol) you use determines the amount of carbon dioxide you emit. So your account would be debited whenever you use fuel with a carbon content, for example at the filling station or when paying the gas bill. There would be a central register at 'QuotaCo'. People who use less than their quota could sell their surplus on the open market to people who wish to use more than theirs.

It was agreed at Kyoto that UK emissions of greenhouse gases must be reduced to 12.5% below the 1990 level by the year 2010. The government, by issuing the right number of units each month, would know that this target would be achieved. It would not have to hope and guess that taxes, subsidies and regulations might achieve the desired result. About half the units would be auctioned to companies and the other half would be divided equally between everyone in the country. This proportion might vary in order to increase the benefit to citizens who avoid using carbon fuels.

Once the carbon units have been issued the market would operate. The family that has a well-insulated house and does not drive a car would have carbon units to sell, while the chief executive, who must fly his private jet, would need to buy units. Thus the market system would allow people to determine their own lifestyle. The government could then concentrate for example, on relieving rural deprivation and helping people insulate their homes.

The system would have three results:

1. Everyone would have a commodity that can be sold, providing him or her with a basic income (see page 60).

2. There would be a built-in tendency towards financial equality because money would flow from those who choose a lavish, carbon-polluting, lifestyle to those who don't.

3. There would be an economic incentive for businesses and individuals to reduce carbon pollution.

The quota would initially be based on present emissions of carbon dioxide and gradually reduce, allowing time for businesses and society to adjust. After the 12.5% reduction has been achieved more reductions will be necessary to bring the UK's emissions to its fair share of what can be sustained globally.

This method could be started immediately, in advance of international agreements, because our Kyoto commitment to a ceiling for carbon emissions is already known.

FACT You would have an allocation of Carbon Units (CU = kilograms of carbon dioxide released) which you could choose to use or sell. The content of fuels is:

Petrol........................2.3 CU per litre
Diesel........................2.4 CU per litre
Natural gas............0.2 CU per kilowatt-hour
Night electricity...0.6 CU per kilowatt-hour
Day electricity.......0.7 CU per kilowatt-hour
The price would be decided by the market.

FACT "Withdrawal from our dependency on fossil fuels will, unquestionably, be the greatest intentional change in technology and the structure of industrial economy ever undertaken, and will require a tremendous collective effort. DTQs could make this happen".
-David Fleming

The Lean Economy
David Fleming
2000

Contraction and Convergence

the logical step after Kyoto

The USA has a convenient excuse for not ratifying the Kyoto protocol: there is no 'substantial participation' by the majority-nations. India and China will be major polluters in the coming years and any agreement, it says, is useless if they are not included in the process. Also, poor nations obviously will not agree to the Kyoto process if their already tiny contribution to carbon dioxide pollution has to be reduced. So is there stalemate?

The Global Commons Institute (GCI) is looking for reconciliation. Let's set out the arguments:

☁ All nations, rich and poor, are in this together and must participate fully.

☁ Greenhouse gas concentrations in the atmosphere must be reduced. The natural 'sinks', such as plants and plankton, which absorb them, can probably only handle 20% - 40% of our present emissions. (These figures may reduce due to deforestation and fires).

☁ Everyone in the world has a right to a fair share of the carrying capacity of the atmosphere. The poor nations will never agree to be second class citizens in perpetuity. Therefore the rich nations either have to agree to a principle of world-wide fairness or plunge the world into runaway global warming. 'Fairness' is, of course, built into the Universal Declaration of Human Rights (and into the US Declaration of Independence). An equal per capita allowance for carbon emissions is the only logical basis for agreement.

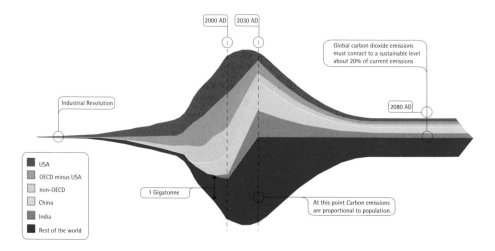 The United States introduced the idea of trading emission 'rights'. This allows flexibility while the consumption of fossil fuel is reduced.

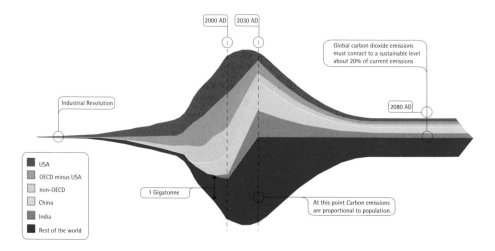 Nations need time to adapt their economies to a level where they are environmentally sustainable.

The GCI has done a computer graph showing *contraction* to an acceptable level of emissions and *convergence* to an equal-per-capita allowance. It considers that politically 'agreeable' targets are:

• contraction to 20% of current emissions by the year 2080,

• convergence to equal-per-capita allowance for carbon dioxide emissions by the year 2030.

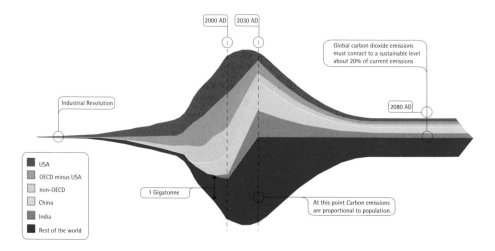

2000 AD 2030 AD

Global carbon dioxide emissions must conract to a sustainable level about 20% of current emissions

Industrial Revolution

2080 AD

USA
OECD minus USA
non-OECD
China
India
Rest of the world

1 Gigatonne

At this point Carbon emissions are proportional to population.

The targets may be adjusted in the light of further scientific understanding. The GCI suggests that Special Emission Rights coupons (SERs) be issued to nations by the International Monetary Fund (IMF). Producers would only be allowed to sell carbon-based fuels once they receive SER coupons. This would be easy to control at the point of fuel-sale, since 80% of all carbon fuel comes from only 122 producers.

The 'Contraction and Convergence' formula therefore provides a scientific and fair framework for intergovernmental agreements on reducing carbon dioxide emissions to a sustainable level.

The formula has been accepted by India, China and most African states. And the Royal Commission on Environmental Pollution says: *"The UK should be prepared to accept the contraction and convergence principle as the basis for international agreement on reducing greenhouse gas emissions".*

Contraction and Convergence
Aubrey Meyer
Schumacher Briefings
Green Books 2000

Making Money

it's really quite simple

You start with £60,000 and call yourself a bank. You lend it to Peter who wants to buy a house. Peter buys the house from Jane, and Jane puts the £60,000 into your bank for safe keeping. You now hold £120,000 (£60K in cash plus £60K secured on a house).

You can now do the same with Michael and you hold £180,000 (the original £60k plus £120k in collateral). Soon you hold a million, most of it in collateral on houses. But you can now attract deposits at low interest to lend to others at high interest. Or you can invest your notional wealth and make money that way. With enough gall you could have started without even the original sum because it was only a paper transaction anyway! The more money you create by putting others into debt, the more interest you can charge. The

banks have always created money, but this system only really took off in Britain with deregulation twenty years ago.

Governments make the notes and coins we use, but this is only 3.6% of the actual 'money' in circulation. The rest, 96.4%, has been created by banks and building societies in the way described above as computer entries, not notes and coins. The money we use daily was created by private institutions, is owned by them and we pay them for using it, not once but year after year. Banks must maintain 10% 'capital adequacy'; they put aside that amount from net interest. It does not inhibit their ability to create yet more capital, it just puts up the cost of borrowing money and keeps them a nice little reserve.

Governments try to control the money supply by putting interest rates up or down. When they are down people borrow more and the money supply rises; then inflation threatens and interest rates go up - people lose their houses, and businesses go bust. This is a subtle form of torture which governments inflict on us.

Businesses in Britain now pay on average 28% of their income to service debt; house 'owners' pay 20% of their's to service their mortgages. This leads to intense competition between companies to advertise and produce cheap, short-lived goods, and for consumers to struggle to remain in employment so that they can pay their mortgages. Western societies are aggressively competitive not because it is in our nature, but because we must be to survive in a world where nearly half of all wealth is creamed off, and the weak go to the wall. We have no choice.

If we work harder and the nation gets wealthier, will our indebtedness reduce? The sad fact is that the reverse happens. In America, a wealthier nation than Britain, 33% of the average household (2 salaries) income is taken by mortgage payments (compared with 20% in the UK). In Japan 'generational mortgages', which extend liability to your children, have been introduced. No wonder the Americans and Japanese work all hours of the day.

Lord Josiah Stamp, former director of the Bank of England, predicted this development in 1937: "The modern banking system manufactures money out of nothing." he said "The process is perhaps the most astounding piece of sleight of hand that was ever invented."

> "To say the financial system is crazy is an understatement. The situation defies description, and it beggars belief that no one involved in the operation takes a long hard look at what they are doing and just bursts out laughing at the innate insanity of the whole process".
> -Michael Rowbotham

Creating New Money
Joseph Huber and James Robertson
New Economics Foundation. 2000
ISBN 1-899407 29 4

Banks

they've got you by the jugular

Our money system is the only one we know. People with money can watch it grow on the stock exchange while they do nothing - it has done so for fifty years and they assume that it will go on doing so. Others pin their hopes on the lottery. Others earn an 'honest crust' and assume that they are being treated fairly. But there have been plenty of other systems. While things are going well, however, any writer criticising the present system is deeply unpopular.

We admire the Americans for their facility with money and commerce, so it is surprising that the most damning criticism of the system came from two of their most revered and intelligent presidents. Thomas Jefferson (1801-09) was alarmed at the development of the banking system. "If the American people ever allow the banks to control the issuance of their currency" he said "they will deprive the people of all property. I sincerely believe that the banking institutions having the power of money are more dangerous to liberty than standing armies".

Abraham Lincoln (1861-65) forged America into one nation. Two main causes of Civil War had been slavery and the financial stranglehold exerted by northern banks over plantations in southern states. Reconciliation was a truly great achievement. Had Lincoln lived longer he might have left an even greater legacy. He wrote a paper called 'Monetary Policy' which might have led to the end of conventional banking and money power in the US, and the world might have followed suit. A major causus belli would have been removed and the bloody history of our age would have been very different. He was assassinated shortly after publishing this document and it was quietly ignored.

Lincoln's 'Monetary Policy' is a masterpiece of clarity; this is a key passage: "the government should not borrow capital at interest as a means of financing government work and public enterprise. The government should create, issue and circulate all the currency and credit needed to satisfy the spending power of the government and the buying power of consumers".

Lincoln's suggestion that money should relate to things that need to be bought and sold seems fairly obvious, but the banks are playing a very profitable game and such suggestions would spoil the fun.

The UK banks got their big chance to create masses of money only twenty years ago after deregulation. The money supply is now three times greater than the value of goods and services available to be bought or sold, and the main commerce in the world is currency speculation, un-taxed, as $1,500 billion flow around the world every day. All the money that exists attracts compound interest, which is nice for the banks but plunges individuals and governments into debt. Many of the highest paid people in the world are the perpetrators of this destructive and unstable game. It is a game that can destroy nations, destroy even banks that get it wrong, and make pawns of us all.

FACT If the UK Central Bank, not commercial banks, created our money supply, the government would receive an additional £47 billion each year, a sixth of its entire tax revenue. This change could not be made if the UK joins the Euro.

The Grip of Death
Michael Rowbotham
Jon Carpenter 1998
ISBN 1-897766-40-8

Economic Growth

and the second law of thermodynamics

Frederick Soddy FRS (1877-1956) was a pioneer atomic scientist who received the Nobel Prize in 1921. He was deeply concerned about atomic power: "If the discovery were made tomorrow" he wrote in 1926 "there is not a nation that would not throw itself heart and soul into the task of applying it to war". The Royal Society ridiculed him for criticising new advances in science. He in turn criticised the Royal Society's comfortable view that scientists have no responsibility for the uses to which science is put.

Soddy considered that the economic system contained built-in elements for conflict and the destruction of Nature once science gave the power, so he applied scientific thought to economics. He was then ridiculed by economists.

Try this: A sack of grain is real and can be considered as 'wealth'. But it reduces. It rots or is eaten by weevils and gradually turns to dust - that is the second law of thermodynamics. But if you talk about 'minus' one sack of grain you are using a mathematical concept: it is Virtual (i.e, conceptual) Wealth, or debt, and it can grow *ad infinitum*. Soddy said that the ruling passion of economists and politicians is to convert wealth that perishes into Virtual Wealth (debt) that lasts (unlike grain) and even grows.

So economists have turned the world on its head: you can store their money and it grows, but if you store something real, like a coat, it decays and gradually loses value. They insist on making the real world of matter, which decays, conform to the purely mathematical concept of growth and compound interest. This is logical nonsense which can only lead to catastrophe in nature and the breakdown of society. To illustrate the absurdity of compound interest Soddy pointed out that if

Christ had invested £1 in our economic system it would now be worth £1,000 billion billion billion billion billion. He said in the 1920s that the result of this non-scientific thinking can only be debt cancellation, revolution or war.

He referred to development since the Industrial Revolution as the 'flamboyant period' of history, when humans are using up the capital stock of coal. This can only be a passing phase, after which we must live 'by sunshine' - which has a maximum rate of flow. Therefore there is a limit to growth. Looking back after 75 years, has he been proved right?

Answer A: Economists might say: "He was an amateur who knew little about our discipline. There has been steady economic growth, wealth has multiplied and our standard of living has increased out of all recognition; our scientific achievements have been spectacular and the whole world is now open to markets, communication and tourism. Through our wealth we have gained the knowledge to deal with whatever problems of health and the environment that may arise. There are, admittedly, still pockets of need but the way to fill them is to ensure further economic growth."

Answer B: Soddy might have replied: "The Wealth of Nature (real wealth) has been eroded. All our gadgets await the ravages of entropy. We have already passed the limit of growth; further economic growth may remove nature's life-support systems entirely. Individual problems with health and the environment will be swamped by general degradation. Virtual Wealth, concentrated in private hands in only a part of the world, has now reached levels that even Soddy could not have imagined and will lead to conflict and the breakdown of society. Economists have created a make-believe world that has nothing to do with the real world. To aim at further economic growth is suicidal."

Which is closer to the truth? Take your pick.

Beyond Growth
Herman Daly
Beacon Press 1996
ISBN 0 8070 4709 0

A Paradox

the history of growth: it makes things worse

Economic growth is a continuing obsession of our government, but a look at history indicates that, far from improving the wellbeing of all citizens, growth can often have the reverse effect. The Index of Sustainable Economic Welfare (ISEW) shows a gradual reduction in the quality of life in the UK over the last twenty-five years though the gross domestic product (GDP) has risen by 50%. With GDP nations prosper by destroying their natural resource base - the costs of disease and disasters are coupled with construction as positive contributions (true!). With ISEW they are negative.   Richard Douthwaite analyses this paradox, devoting a chapter to each of the statements below: If you instinctively question these provocative statements, try reading his arguments in full.

🌱 Capitalism cannot survive without growth. Firms are compelled to expand to avoid collapse. In the world up to 1914, this compulsion built empires, destroyed indigenous cultures and, finally, led to world war.

🌱 Growth in Britain during the Agricultural and Industrial Revolutions made life progressively worse for ordinary people until about 1850. Conditions then began to improve - but as a result of depression, not growth. By 1914 living conditions might, just, have returned to their level of two hundred years previously.

🌱 Major advances in the living conditions of the British people resulted from two world wars, the depressions of the twenties and thirties and the freely redistributive policies of the 1945 Labour government. Whenever growth appeared, life for the majority got worse.

🌱 Because Mrs. Thatcher sought to accelerate growth by improving investors' returns, her three governments engineered a major shift in the distribution of incomes and wealth in favour of the better-off.

🌱 The growth process perverts the national economy within which it works. It causes unemployment and makes labour less affordable. It enables the concentration of economic power and requires ever-higher shares of the national income to be spent by the state.

🌱 It was not until 1955 that accelerating the growth rate became the major British economic obsession. Since then, the methods used to generate higher levels of output have caused a large increase in chronic illness.

🌱 All the indicators of the quality of life show that it deteriorated in Britain between 1955 and 1988. Unemployment, for example, soared and crime increased eightfold.

🌱 Because their need for growth forces firms to adopt new technologies before their impact can be assessed, environmental disasters such as large-scale release of CFCs and PCBs are inevitable.

🌱 Politicians consider economic growth more important than keeping the world fit for human habitation.

Douthwaite concludes that the only sustainable society is a stable society - history and logic show that there is no such thing as sustainable growth.

FACT Nature provides the model for a stable system. It has delightful and infinite variety; its complexity increases with time; when things go wrong it finds corrections or alternatives; it gradually turns dust into things of value; it captures pollution and lays it down into the earth's crust. But nature has no net growth. It is stable. It provides wonders on a finite planet.

To say that a stable economy is not possible simply shows the poverty of our imagination.

The Growth Illusion
(1999 edition)
Richard Douthwaite
Green Books Ltd
ISBN 1 870098 76 5

Citizen's Income

for a civilized civilization

People no longer have a job for life - they expect change. This is exhilarating, and it suits modern business to have flexibility. Productivity must increase and industry must not be loaded with commitments to staff.

Any civilized government must ensure that its citizens don't starve, so a safety net is essential. We achieve this through humiliation and stress: if you don't get a job on leaving school or university you join the dole queue; if you supplement the meager benefit allowance, you are 'cheating the system'. Thousands are caught in the poverty and unemployment traps that discourage initiative. When you lose your job you fall into mortgage debt and may lose your house. Life has never been more stressful. It is a barbarous system.

The government's answer is growth. Create more jobs and make citizens into job-seekers. It is a stale policy that has been limping along for the last eighty years. At its heart is a fundamental fault highlighted in the 1920s: when economists were crying out for growth in order to increase employment, it was pointed out that there were already plenty of goods being produced but no one could afford to buy them. So why try to get out of the Depression by making yet more goods with cut-throat competition?

That is when the idea of a Citizen's Income started. If people have money to spend, business will flourish - use the carrot not the stick. A Citizen's Income would be paid by the Government unconditionally to all individuals independent of other income, and without any requirement to work. It would be enough to meet basic needs. The rate would be higher for adults than children and higher for the elderly than for those of working age. It would be every citizen's by right, not as charity or as a 'benefit'.

How on earth can this be afforded?

Funding could be afforded thus:

• a Citizen's Income would replace the expensive benefit and tax allowance system. This is currently so elaborate that its abolition would release about half the necessary funds.

• the Domestic Tradable Quota could halve the amount that would need to be distributed as a Citizen's Income (see page 46).

However it could accompany other changes that would raise revenue, and are anyway necessary to achieve sustainability:

• VAT on non-essential items of consumption should be increased in order to discourage excessive use of global resource,

• carbon tax should become the main source of government revenue - to combat global warming, (it would reduce or replace income tax)

• the Central Bank should issue all money; this would raise about a sixth of the government's revenue and abolish the public sector borrowing requirement.

A Citizen's Income would provide people with a financial platform from which they can either choose to earn as much as possible or from which they can choose to do work that satisfies them, even if it is poorly paid. Employers (and employment) would benefit because of lower staff costs - they would only need to top up income - so they could employ more staff.

Would there be no incentive to work?
For some - but some are already out of work in a system that discourages them from keeping their skills alive. Most of us want to earn more than our neighbours.

Would society fall apart?
Unlikely. Sociologists are more likely to trace the seeds of antisocial behaviour to the social and financial exclusion which is induced by the present system.

The Citizen's Income would remove much of the stress of modern life. It would provide business with flexibility. It would remove the poverty and employment traps. It would enable people to choose activities that are creative and develop their skills; it would integrate work with social contact and a feeling of belonging; it would remove the separation of 'work' and 'leisure'. The western concepts of work, job and employment are not universal – many languages do not even have words for these separate concepts.

A citizen's income would do more than anything else to give us a humane and civilized society.

Transforming Economic Life
James Roberston
Schumacher Briefing
Green Books 1998
ISBN 1 870098 72 2

Wörgl

money that is not worth keeping

Have you ever wondered at the beauty of buildings from the twelfth and thirteenth centuries in southern Europe, when about 600 new towns were built with solid stone houses that have survived to this day? Ironically, it was not a politically stable period. The wars waged by the Church on the Cathars necessitated much reconstruction. It was partly about religion and partly about money - the Church's potential loss of revenue. Inadvertently a rather strange system of money was responsible for the reconstruction that gives us such pleasure today.

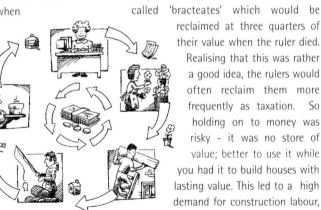

In the Holy Roman Empire rulers of the dozens of small independent states issued thin silver coins called 'bracteates' which would be reclaimed at three quarters of their value when the ruler died. Realising that this was rather a good idea, the rulers would often reclaim them more frequently as taxation. So holding on to money was risky - it was no store of value; better to use it while you had it to build houses with lasting value. This led to a high demand for construction labour, so wages were good; working hours were short, about six hours a day; and there were at least ninety religious holidays a year. It greatly improved the quality of life and was wonderful for the local economy.

But when gold coins were introduced in the fifteenth century it became worth storing money because of the amount of precious metal it contained; you could keep it under your mattress rather than use it. So demand for labour dropped, wages fell, unemployment appeared, some businesses closed down because people could earn more by lending the money they had accumulated on interest rather than by trading. And, to cap it all, rulers had to find other means of taxation.

The idea of issuing money that is not worth storing has cropped up frequently since. Wörgl, a small town in Austria, was suffering from the Depression in the 1930s. There was 35% unemployment and local taxes were seriously in arrears, crippling the work of the council. The mayor negotiated a loan from a credit union bank and printed scrip notes. These were guaranteed against the national currency though you only got 98% of their value if you exchanged them. You had to stamp each note monthly to 1% of its value, so it cost you to keep it and you used it as quickly as possible. Half the council's staff wages were paid in the scrip and the mayor allowed local taxes to be paid in scrip, so businesses were prepared to accept it. The effect was to stimulate local trade, tax arrears were paid off and there was full employment. The council was able to employ 50 extra people, paying their wages entirely in scrip, to repair and surface streets, and to extend the sewerage system. Then they built a ski jump and a reservoir without incurring any debt.

Not surprisingly, other towns started to copy the scheme. The Central Bank, alarmed that it was losing control of the money system, took out legal proceedings and closed it down thirteen months after it started.

Many similar schemes were started in the US, with the same response from banks. In March 1933 President Roosevelt forbade any further scrip issues, being advised that the financial system was being taken out of the government's hands - by the people!

Short Circuit
Richard Douthwaite
Green Books 1996
ISBN 1 870098 64 1

A New World Order

four currencies

Anyone who takes part in a baby-sitting circle uses an alternative currency. It may be IOU chits, entries in a diary or just a mental note. There is nothing odd about multiple currencies. It is very odd, however, to use just one currency for speculating on the international money market, buying cabbages, and saving for your old age. Richard Douthwaite suggests four currency systems, each designed for a specific purpose:

⑤ an *international currency* for trading between nations;

⑤ a *national-exchange currency* for trading within a nation,

⑤ various *user-controlled currencies*, and

⑤ a *store-of-value currency* for your savings.

The *international currency*, would be an energy-backed-currency-unit, an 'ebcu', and take its value from the right to emit greenhouse gases. There is no international currency at present:

various national ones such as the dollar, the pound sterling and the Swiss Franc are used instead. As these are debt-based and not linked to anything real, the global economy is extremely unstable.

To get the new currency going, the IMF would issue each country with 'ebcus' in proportion to its 1990 population. No more would ever be issued. A nation's existing wealth would remain in its other currencies. Then, each month, the IMF would issue coupons called Special Emission Rights (SERs) to each country on the same population basis. These coupons would confer the right to emit a certain amount of greenhouse gas and would be handed in whenever fossil fuel was purchased. Each year, the number of SERs issued to each country would fall so that, within a few decades, the total amount of greenhouse gas the world released would match the earth's capacity to absorb it.

National governments would decide how many of their SER coupons to distribute internally to enable their citizens to use fossil energy, and how many to trade internationally. India, which uses little energy at present, would have surplus SERs to sell. The US would use all its coupons internally and need to purchase more on the international market, using its 'ebcus' in payment.

The *national-exchange currency* would be for buying and selling within a country, but not as a store for one's long-term savings. If trade increased, the central bank would print more of this currency and spend it into circulation, thus reducing the government's tax needs. This might cause mild inflation but this is fine because it induces you to use money before it loses value, thus encouraging trade and employment.

The national-exchange currency would be supplemented by a wide range of *user-controlled currencies* such as Local Exchange Trading Schemes (LETS), Time Dollars and systems modeled on the Swiss Wirtschaftsring.

The *store-of-value currency* would be a fixed quantity of a special form of money used only for purchasing and selling capital assets. If more houses or shares were traded, for example, the need for this currency, and hence its value, would rise in relation to the national-exchange currency. So:

⑨ The international-currency would keep the world economy within the carrying capacity of the planet.

⑨ The *national-exchange currency* and many *user-controlled currencies* would encourage economic activity within a nation.

⑨ The *store-of-value currency* would link your savings to the prosperity of the country – no more and no less.

Other thinkers suggest incremental change. But, should there be a global collapse, it might be better to adopt Douthwaite's radical proposals than to try and patch up our present perverse financial system.

The Ecology of Money
Richard Douthwaite
Green Books 1999
ISBN 1 870098 81 1

'Them' or 'Us'

a Gandhian approach

Henry VIII is usually credited with creating our centralised system of government. Everything now flows from central government - social benefits, money for improving property, and other grants. Gandhi suggested precisely the opposite. Various projects in India are applying his principle: that the local community, at grass-roots level, should be the basic unit of government.

Seventy-five villages at Lathur, in South India, have been identified as being below the poverty line and in need of aid. But it is the village (100 to 300 people), not the authority, which decides which individuals are in need and how the aid should be distributed. The village council of 20 men and 20 women is elected annually and the post of headperson rotates.

Mr Rajamani could double his income if his well were deeper. He applied to the village council. The village council assessed his proposal and approved the necessary loan (from the authority). He repaid the loan plus interest to the village council, not to the authority. This is the route by which aid flows to the village community.

98% of loans are satisfactorily repaid, and the failures are usually for a particular reason that can be understood by the village council. So the community builds up a fund. Once the fund reaches a certain size the authority withdraws and the village itself continues with the process using its own accumulated funds. After five years, thirty-five of the villages now require no further aid. A community bank, controlled by the village councils, handles the funds.

It is necessary, of course, to ensure that each village keeps to the system and is not bullied by a few individuals or taken over by a political group. This is done, not by the authority, but at an annual two-day gathering of all the villages. In addition to the business in hand this gathering becomes a festival, a place of contact and even a marriage market. It is the lowest tier of the state electoral system that Gandhi recommended, where each tier takes responsibility for its own affairs and aims to determine the policy of higher tiers of authority. The higher authority must be the servant of the lower. In other words, the villager is the maker of his/her own destiny, and is his/her own legislator, through his/her chosen representative. The ultimate storehouse of his/her power, should other means fail, is non-violent civil disobedience.

thousands of individuals. Local authorities are reluctant to allow a street community to decide how its road might be allocated between children and cars, or to approve the design of new buildings; to set up its own arrangements for repairs, and re-cycling of waste and water; or to combine with adjacent communities to provide its own school or clinic. A street community in Hull secretly grassed its road overnight for the Jubilee in 1977 and had it ripped up by the authority the following week – it took twenty years for them to get it back to grass through official channels. Citizens only really feel involved, and thus committed, when they themselves make the decisions that vitally affect them. There is a fundamental difference between decisions made by 'US' and decisions made by 'THEM'.

In Britain, power is held by a small group at the top, subject only to occasional elections - a system we call democracy, though a political analyst would call it elective oligarchy. Each tier distrusts the one below, so rules and regulations abound. The lowest tier of local authority controls

It is no wonder that social exclusion has become a major issue in Britain. When people cannot determine their own destiny the community falls apart. The vital step is from mere 'consultation' to the exercise of proper citizen power through participation. This requires the management of budgets by communities that are small enough for all to be involved - street scale communities. This is democracy.

A very hopeful sign in the UK is the New Deal for Communities programme. The government allocates, say, £50 million on a ten year programme, and the community (not the local authority), from street committees upwards, decides how it shall be used. Paid 'animaters' are chosen by the committees to facilitate the process.

"Freedom is to be attained by educating the people to a sense of their capacity to regulate and control authority".
Mohendas Gandhi.

Participation Works!
New Economics Foundation
1999
ISBN 1 899407 17 0

Wealth in Poverty

a tribal's view

Wealth means different things to different people. For tribals, money has little meaning. It is 'community' that they value.

The community at Gudalur, South India, is extremely poor. They used to live in the forest but could not prove ownership of any land. In their culture, there was no conception that land *could* be owned. Land, water and air are regarded as commons, available for all to use.

The government sold the forests in which the tribal community lived to Brooke Bond. It was assumed that the forests were empty, and Brook Bond acquired large tracts of them as tea plantations. Tribals continued to live on the edges. But how could they secure their rights? The only way was to plant permanent crops.

But when they did so the foresters pulled up the crops and destroyed their homes.

In 1984 Stan and Mari Thekaekara, social activists, persuaded five of these tribes, totaling 5,000 families, to act together. When individuals were threatened, the community gathered to protest. They secured land for some, but ownership of individual plots did not help the community.

The tribals decided that the only way to strengthen the community was to obtain a plantation. They prepared a business plan and, with Stan's help, obtained the loan to buy it. The plantation is now their own. In two years the yield doubled, and it now supports a school and a hospital. From being virtual outcasts, the tribals are now respected.

Their tea fetches high prices because of its quality but, rather than dividing the profits among the group working on the plantation, the pickers themselves said that any extra earnings should go to the community. They said that if they became wealthy while others remained poor, their community would fall apart.

Mari said: "The Adivasis (tribals) were clear about their wealth. 'It is our community, our children, our unity, our culture, the forest'. Money was not mentioned. We, the non-adivasis, were stunned. As we discussed concepts of poverty further, we realised that they didn't see themselves as poor. They saw themselves as people without money".

Stan and Mari visited the Easterhouse estate in Glasgow as part of a North-South exchange and the question of poverty again forced itself upon them. In Glasgow everyone had a television, running water, heating and benefit payments. The Adivasis would regard these things as inconceivable luxuries. "But most of the men in Easterhouse hadn't had a job in 20 years." Mari said. "They were dispirited, depressed, often alcoholic. Their self-esteem had gone. Emotionally and mentally they were far worse off than the poor at Gudalur, though the physical trappings of poverty were less stark".

Stan and Mari brought a group of Adivasis to Germany. The gift they valued most from their hosts was being treated as equals - something they did not experience at home. But they were speechless when they saw an old people's home. "How can children send their old parents to live alone. We must ensure that such things never happen in our society, no matter how much we progress". Then Karl, their German host, came home one evening preoccupied with the news that he might lose his job. Bomman, the Adivasi, worried all night for his new German friend. "I have an idea", he announced in the morning, "I can make bamboo flutes when I go home and Karl can sell them here till he finds a job". Through contacts like these the Adivasis now trade directly with their friends in Europe.

When a group was next threatened with eviction, it was the contact with their friends in Germany that persuaded Brook Bond to concede - confrontation might damage their image internationally. The tribals had found that community, with its ability to empower, even when up against a trans-national company, can be extended across the world.

FACT Free trade can hurt. A letter we received from Stan in July 2000 said: "one of the most unfortunate issues has been the drop in price of both tea and coffee in the local market. The government has opened up the Indian market and large imports are being allowed. This has created a fall in the price for producers while the price in shops remains the same".

"There is no quiet place in the white man's cities. What is there to life if a man cannot hear the lonely cry of the whippoowill or the arguments of the frogs around the pond at night?"
Chief Seattle

Dream Scheme
Mari Marcel-Thekaekara
New Internationalist
April 2000

A Great American Idea

odious debt

It appears that international law has one rule for the strong and another rule for the weak.

The concept known as 'odious debt' was established by the United States in 1898. America had captured Cuba but found that their new colony had large debts to Spanish banks. The US refused to pay these debts, arguing that the debts had been 'imposed upon the people of Cuba without their consent and by force of arms'. Thus the doctrine that neither the people of a country nor its new government are responsible for the 'odious debts' of a previous regime, was established. However, do you imagine that in recent years, the poor nations have been allowed to invoke this doctrine? Certainly not!

South African apartheid was defined by the United Nations as a 'crime against humanity'. When Nelson Mandela became president, he and the people of South Africa inherited more than $18 billion in debts. Surely no debts could be described as more odious! But the IMF warned that unless the debts were repaid, however odious, South Africa would be isolated by the international community. Money that should have been used to build schools and homes, to create jobs and to repair the environment, instead was sent to the US, UK and Swiss banks that had financed apartheid.

Mobuto, dictator of Zaire, was a friend of the North and the North lent him money. He was known as the 'kleptocrat' because of his lavish palaces and purchases from Europe. When he died in 1998 he left debts of $13 billion. Zaire is now the Democratic Republic of Congo and the West wants its money back. The new government should be spending every penny on rebuilding the shattered country. Instead, every man, woman and child in the country must repay $260 in debt.

Investors lent the Philippine's Marcos regime the money to build the Bataan nuclear power station, and Westinghouse (a US company) channeled millions of dollars of bribes through Swiss banks to secure the contract. It was in an earthquake zone so was never used. The Marcos' personal wealth was $10 billion but it is the Philippine government that must pay the debt.

Poor countries, it seems, must pay their debts, however odious. But Long Term Capital Management, a US-based 'hedge fund', was treated with concerned sympathy when it landed itself in debt. The Federal Reserve immediately found $3.6 billion to bail out its friend.

Dealing with the Asian crisis, the IMF declared that 'reducing expectation of bailouts must be the first step in restructuring Asia's financial markets'. Asian companies were bankrupted and became rich pickings for northern companies. However the IMF ultimately agreed $120 billion funds to be made available to pay Asian debts to - whom? To northern banks, of course. Thus the North not only took over Asian businesses at knock-down rates, it also got its money back.

The guiding principle for the IMF and the World Bank is this: whatever happens, whoever is at fault, the wealth of western creditors must be protected and enhanced.

Take the Hit
Joseph Hanlon
New Internationalist
May 1999

Third World Debt

view from the North

Poor nations owe us a lot of money, $2,500 billion to be exact. Of this, $200 billion is owed by 41 Heavily Indebted Poor Countries (HIPCs). The HIPC debt is small compared with the total, and some of it is being 'forgiven' following the successful campaign by the pressure group Jubilee 2000.

The World Bank President, Mr Wolfensohn, said "the notion that for the Jubileum someone can come along and forgive that debt is whimsical. If you have a society based on debt forgiveness, who's going to invest in debt anymore? So you really screw up the market". (sic)

The First World, goes the Northern view, gave aid and loans in order to help Third World countries develop their economies, and to combat poverty and disease. In addition the World Bank has been providing health, education and agricultural advisers. The Agrochemical Revolution, pioneered by First World scientists, greatly increased productivity since the 1950s and helped developing countries adopt modern techniques to replace traditional farming methods. Much of the aid was squandered by corrupt regimes and many countries mishandled their economies. With this perspective, the First World argues that it has made serious efforts to help developing countries rise out of poverty.

But northern governments and the World Bank can be accused of gross malpractice. If a high-street bank lends to a corrupt or chaotic company which then goes bust, the bank loses its money and must write off the debt. But the North knowingly lends to countries that cannot possibly pay back the capital, let alone the interest. It also lends to corrupt regimes for political reasons. The debts are calculated in 'hard' currency, usually dollars, so they increase in real terms as the local currency devalues. On top of this the debts attract compound interest. But the North never writes off the bad debts from its books - they accumulate and multiply. So the total Third World debt is many times the amount actually lent.

The money owed by HIPCs to commercial banks was miraculously converted by the G7 (group of seven northern nations) into debt owed to public institutions, like the International Monetary Fund (IMF); and through them to taxpayers. You and I must now pick up the tab for the malpractice of commercial banks. The cynicism and immorality of this is absolutely staggering – the G7 were prepared to release commercial banks from their debt but not the HIPCs who had to divert money from health, education and poverty alleviation.

Nicaragua's health budget is a quarter of the amount it spends on servicing debt. Mali repays more than it spends on health (and one in four of its children die before the age of five). Zambia's repayments are greater than its spending on health and education. Throughout the majority nations, debt repayments cripple struggling economies and cause death through malnutrition. Should a dictator adopt the policies imposed by the IMF he would be accused of genocide.

By contrast, the financial assets of northern banks grow at the rate of $2,500 billion a year – the amount of the entire third world debt! As for aid - debt repayments by the Third World are nine times as much as the aid it receives.

At a meeting in Cologne in June 1999 the G7 made a gesture to the HIPCs, 'forgiving' debts to the tune of $100 billion. Campaigners were jubilant and there was dancing in the streets.

They had forgotten that the IMF and the World Bank were involved. These require 'structural adjustments' before money is released - measures like opening markets to international trade. (Guess who benefits). A year after Cologne, only $2 billion additional debt reductions had been made. Not a single country had had its debt cancelled, and the debt of only five countries had been reduced (Nicaragua, Mali and Zambia were not among these). Tanzania benefited - its annual debt re-payments were reduced from $162 to $150 million (it spends $87 million on health).

Third World economies are largely dependent on selling commodities - raw mined minerals and crops. But WTO policies of free and open markets are pushing the price of commodities to an all time low. This is wonderful for the rich First World (it is one reason the US has a current account surplus), but it is devastating for the Third World.

FACT A strong nation like India could set a precedent by refusing to repay 'restructured' debts (as opposed to normal business transactions). The interest they have paid is more than the original debt. Rich nations would, of course, threatened sanctions. Expatriate Indians might then underwrite any threatened loss to the government, as they did when India successfully averted sanctions after nuclear tests. And, anyway, the US might hesitate to impose sanctions when much of its accountancy is done overnight in Bangalore.

FACT Annual expenditure on health per capita:

US	$2,765
Tanzania	$ 4

FACT Between 1503 and 1660, 185 thousand kilos of gold and 16 million kilos of silver were transferred from Central America to Europe. One would hesitate to accuse Europe of looting or stealing; it was surely a loan. If central American nations only ask for modest interest, half of what we now charge the poor Third World, the debt we now owe them would have 300 digits.

"IMF rescue packages are intended only to rescue western creditors".
Ellen Frank. Professor of Economics, Boston.

Jubilee 2000 Coalition
www.jubilee2000uk.org
mail@jubilee2000uk.org

First World Debt

view from the South

Money is not the only form of wealth. Would you envy a billionaire his money if he were locked in a prison cell? If we can't enjoy the world around us we are indeed poor. So there are two kinds of wealth: your money and your environment. There are also two kinds of debt - the money you owe and the damage you have done to the environment.

The First World says it is owed money. Lots of it, plus compound interest. And not in devalued rupee, baht or rouble but in hard western dollars, so the original debt may now be multiplied by five or ten times due to devaluation and compound interest.

The Third World, eighty percent of the world population, has a very different view about debt. They are asking:

Who has been using up the earth's fossil fuel, mineral and timber resources?

 Who has been polluting the atmosphere with greenhouse gases thus causing hurricanes and rising sea levels that devastate the South?

Who has been profiting from the chemicals that have got into the food chain, degraded our soil and poisoned our aquifers?

Who has been over-fishing the oceans and depriving poor countries of their off-shore fisheries?

How dare the First World require us to make 'structural adjustments' to our economies when it makes no structural adjustment to the environmental damage it is causing throughout the world?

They say that the First World has a massive debt to other nations for depleting the natural capital of the world, but this debt is fundamentally different from the Third World Debt. Financial capital claimed by the First World is artificial; it is a human invention which is meant to conform to rules largely invented by the First World. Natural capital, on the other hand, is real and finite. It is the fossil resource fixed in the earth's crust through millions of years of photosynthesis; it is the constant daily flow of energy from the sun; it is the ability of the atmosphere to keep the earth pleasant and habitable.

The Third World could have a case in law against the First World. If pollution by the industrialised nations has led to climate instability which is causing drought and famine in the Horn of Africa, sinking island states, causing flooding in Venezuela, Bangladesh, Orissa and Mozambique - the industrialised nations should pay compensation. Attempts to quantify this liability have an air of fantasy - you can quantify loss of infrastructure but how do you quantify loss of life, loss of livelihood, loss of culture? The debt is infinitely greater than the whole of the Third World financial debt.

Law is the Northern approach to resolving conflict. But applying systems of legal justice in these circumstances will simply lead to endless conflict while the world slips into catastrophe.

Many Southern nations have a different system of resolving conflict: looking for common ground. The South is looking for a just and fair world economy. The North is dependent on environmental stability. The First World minority must humbly ask the majority nations of the Third World to share the damage it has caused. The Third World is asking for confrontation to be put behind us and - please - stop thinking of everything in terms of money. We must work together to save the world from environmental catastrophe and to eradicate hunger.

"Only when the last tree has died and the last river been poisoned and the last fish been caught will we realise that we cannot eat money".
A Native American

FACT The World Disasters Report 2000 calculates that the rich nations have amassed a climate debt of $13,000 billion which is growing at an increasing rate. This is currently more than five times the total Third World Debt.

FACT 96% of deaths from natural disasters occur in developing countries.

FACT Industrialised countries generate over 62 times more carbon dioxide per person than the least developed countries.

"The disaster in Mozambique is consistent with IPCC predictions and is consistent with what we must now expect with climate change".
Sir John Houghton
Director-General of the UK Met Office.

Who Owes Who?
Christian Aid 1999
PO Box 100
London SE1 7RT

The World Trade Organisation

dull but important

The December 1999 World Trade Organisation (WTO) conference in Seattle was a fiasco. Protesters took to the streets and delegates failed to agree on anything. The cover of The Economist carried a picture of a refugee child with the caption 'the real losers from Seattle' - an emotional accusation that the protesters were harming the very people they claimed to champion. The WTO maintains that free trade between nations, unhindered by protective barriers, will increase global wealth and help developing countries to rise out of poverty. It suits the rich also: "I do not believe" said President Clinton "that a country with 4.5% of the world's people can maintain its standard of living if we don't have more customers".

The WTO in 1995 supervised one of the most important economic developments of the last fifty years – the progressive removal of barriers to trade. It has been remarkably successful; the proportion of global domestic product (GDP) traded internationally has risen from 5% in 1946 to 25% now.

But something has gone wrong - as international trade has increased, the gap between rich and poor in the world has also increased. Poverty is now so desperate that many of the poorer nations cannot afford to protect their environment, adopt basic health care, or monitor labour conditions. More people are hungry than ever before in the history of the world.

The WTO is housed in grandiose premises on the shores of Lake Geneva. It is advised by hundreds of experts and lawyers. It takes advice on food safety from the Codex Alimentarius Commission, a body largely consisting of people from the food industry, which meets in secret. Poor countries cannot afford to keep delegates in expensive Switzerland; cannot keep up with the mountains of documents which may hide crucial information; cannot send experts and lawyers; and so cannot effectively represent their case.

Under WTO rules governments are not allowed to: favour local firms, prevent foreigners having a controlling interest in local companies, favour trade partners, or subsidise domestic industry (though it turns a blind eye to the massive subsidies the US and EU give to their farmers, who export to poor countries).

WTO rules favour transnational companies which benefit from economies of scale, which can undercut to capture a market, which are immune to local consumer feed-back, and which can shift their production whenever it suits them to countries with lower wages and fewer environmental or labour regulations. In all these

fields local manufacturers, suppliers and retailers are at a disadvantage.

The WTO promotes free trade, and free trade is based on the classical theory of 'comparative advantage' - a country benefits from selling what it grows or makes better or more cheaply than other countries. That theory worked when capital was stationary, but now corporations simply take over the profitable businesses of poor countries leaving the nationals even poorer.

The riots in Seattle in December 1999 were a clear indication that WTO policies are perceived as favouring transnational corporations to the detriment of poor nations. Civil society is saying that laissez-faire economics is unacceptable, and corporations must be subject to standards set by national governments for social wellbeing, health and environmental protection. The WTO should be closed and trade should be regulated through the United Nations.

FACT WTO aims to weaken national governments and promote free trade. Why? Think about the needs of the rich industrialised nations and it becomes clear:

• The North has few raw materials of its own so must obtain these from poor nations. If poor countries had strong governments they would club together to protect their assets. Therefore take power away from governments.

• The North produces more goods than are necessary to meet its own needs, so it must cultivate markets elsewhere. Therefore the majority nations' markets must be opened for trade.

The World Trade System
Friends of the Earth
FoE International
foeint.@antenna.nl

Free Trade

winners and losers

We all love bananas. But they have a story to tell, too.

The European Union imported 8% of its bananas from Caribbean countries under favourable terms. The World Trade Organisation (WTO) stopped this and told the EU to buy 'American' bananas.

Alroy Smart is a loser. He has a decent little farm in St Lucia growing bananas, but he will lose it. "The situation is really bad now" he said "what to do? There is no alternative. Bananas were the only thing that we could depend on". There will now be mass unemployment.

But farmers on the other side of the dispute, in central America, will lose too. Labour, health and environmental standards on these plantations are appallingly low - workers get just three cents for every dollar earned exporting bananas, and that won't change.

There are other losers in this banana war, like Arran Aromatics, the main employer on a Scottish island. There is no reason why it should be victimised, it has nothing to do with bananas, but the WTO has authorised the US to impose sanctions on its products. Forty percent of its turnover is affected. Many other unrelated small businesses in Europe are similar losers.

So who gains in this trade war?

Chiquita, the multinational banana company, donated $500,000 to the US Democratic Party funds, and a few days later the Clinton/Gore administration filed a complaint to the WTO on behalf of Chiquita. The WTO only allows local or company experts to appear before its tribunals, and the Caribbean nations had none, so were not represented. No one was surprised when the WTO ruled in favour of the US. Chiquita then donated $350,000 to Republican Party funds, and

Congress, controlled by Republicans, imposed crippling tariffs on goods imported from the EU as punishment for continuing their favoured trade with the Caribbean. By these means, Chiquita was the winner.

The WTO has never yet ruled in favour of society, health or the environment in preference to free trade. But the World Bank and the IMF do not believe in free trade or economic determinism when it affects First World banking: witness their massive intervention when the Japanese financial system faced meltdown. However they force this cruel system on the poor and vulnerable.

The E.U. considers hormone treatment cruel to cattle and possibly carcinogenic to consumers of beef. The WTO has ruled against the EU in the interests of free trade and the US is allowed to put 'revenge' sanctions on products like Roquefort cheese.

In the Philippines 500,000 corn farmers risk losing their livelihoods because, under free trade rules, cheaper corn from America must be imported. America and Europe subsidise their farmers by about £20,000 a year, a hundred times a Filipino grower's entire income.

A few of the other free trade 'successes' are:
- the scrapping of US regulations to protect turtles and porpoises,
- forcing Canada to market a fuel additive which it believes causes psychosis, memory loss and early death,
- preventing legislation to ban animal leg-traps,
- preventing legislation to ban cosmetics testing on animals,
- protecting companies trading with Myanmar. (Had this principle been established earlier and applied to South Africa, Nelson Mandela would probably still be in prison.)
- preventing Thailand, concerned at the massive increase in young smokers, from banning cigarette imports.

On top of all the above, the increase in cross-border trade has created an exponential growth in air and road freight throughout the world with related accident, health, congestion and climatic effects. The WTO does nothing to address these problems. We are all losers.

A success story?

Free trade has been successful in reducing global commodity prices. This has great benefit for rich importing countries who can now pay off their national debts. It is a disaster for poor nations with little else to sell.

Between 1980 and 1997 commodity prices dropped:

Sugar down 73%;
coffee down 64%;
cocoa down 58%;
rubber down 52%;
rice down 51%;
cotton down 43%;
tea down 36%;
copper down 30%.

1999 commodity prices were lower than ever... good news for coffee drinkers, dreadful for the poor coffee producers.

FACT One US company, Cargill, controls 80% of global grain distribution.

FACT The top ten corporations control:
85% of all pesticides
60% of all veterinary medicine
35% of all pharmaceuticals
32% of all commercial seed

FACT It has been estimated that US corporations receive $2,400 billion annually in subsidies and 'external' costs like the use of roads, all provided by the taxpayer. This is equal to the entire Third World Debt.

Market Whys and Wherefores
David Jenkins
Cassell 1999
ISBN 0 304 70608 6

Basic Needs

isn't everyone as happy as we are?

Helena Norberg-Hodge worked in Ladakh, in the Himalayas, one of the harshest climates in the world, scorched by the sun in summer and frozen for eight months of the year. She noted the immense care taken over the use of minimal resources, relying on the outside world only for salt and tea - there was literally no waste. Ladakhis worked hard in the summer but at their own rate, accompanied by laughter and song; the distinction between work and play was fluid. Winter was a time for festivals, parties and story-telling.

After visiting this poorest of countries for sixteen years she said "their sense of joy seems so firmly anchored within them that circumstances cannot change it. At first I couldn't believe that the Ladakhis could be as happy as they appeared. It took a long time to accept that the smiles I saw were real". Is this 'noble savage' romanticism or do we need to be more precise in defining human needs?

Manfred Max-Neef, a specialist in human-scale development, identifies nine basic needs:

- **Subsistence -** *Creation, health, food, shelter skills, work, feedback*
- **Protection -** *security, society*
- **Affection -** *friendship, family, love*
- **Understanding -** *curiosity, education*
- **Participation -** *responsibilities, interaction, community*
- **Leisure -** *play, fantasy, intimacy, privacy*
- **Creation -** *skills, work, feedback*
- **Identity -** *belonging, groups, recognition*
- **Freedom -** *autonomy, rights, dissent*

But basic human needs can be satisfied in very different ways by different cultures. If we propose to make changes to the economic system of a country, we should check how the changes are likely to affect any one of these nine basic needs. To facilitate this he discusses each need against four aspects of living: what we are; what we have; what we do; how we interact.

Severe deprivation in one need may paralyse all other considerations. This is particularly the case with hunger (subsistence) which paralyses 13% of the world population. But the same is true of other needs. Social exclusion in an affluent society may lead to criminal behaviour. Total lack of affection or loss of identity may lead even wealthy people to suicide.

For politicians and bureaucrats the concept of basic human needs is usually limited to food, health and education - to be met through aid and advice handed down from international agencies. They see only the economic goods, which represent a fraction of real needs, and are surprised when these cause havoc in countries with a strong spiritual and traditional culture.

For Max-Neef human-scale development comes from the grass roots. An economic strategy may satisfy one need and not another. If it causes extreme deprivation to any one of the needs it must be abandoned however beneficial it appears to be in other respects. Development will be destructive unless those involved participate fully.

Back to Ladakh: globalisation may bring them additional income. But the influx of money and consumer perishables may simply make them aware of the deprivations of an extreme climate while destroying a culture that in the past has satisfied all their fundamental human needs.

FACT In 1995 it rained in Ladakh for the first time in living memory. Their houses are built for a dry climate. Climate change? They have done nothing to deserve this.

From the Outside Looking In
Max-Neef
Zed Books 1992
ISBN 1 856491 88 9

Feeding the World

a risky business

There are many things you can do without, but not food. Industrialised agriculture is, ironically, putting our food security at risk.

At the beginning of the last century, food was largely grown and distributed locally and most people made their living off the land. At its end the food trade had become a major global business, dominated by just twenty companies. In spite of this, half the population of poor countries are still in farming families. So, to give security to half the world, the first priority should be to ensure that they are not forced off the land, that they are not made dependent on seed purchase, that their water source is secure, that they are helped with appropriate research and appropriate technology, and that their market is not undercut by subsidised crops from elsewhere.

In the last fifty years, global crop production has more than doubled. Yet two-fifths of the world population are malnourished, the highest proportion ever. Half of these are hungry. The other half are malnourished because they eat too much. This is not surprising because most research is now funded by, and for, industrial agribusinesses. It is in their interest to develop and advertise food that will appeal to the rich, not the poor. It is in their interest to encourage growing for export, not to meet local needs. It is in their interest to make farmers dependent on purchasing their seed, chemicals, and machinery - not to be self-sufficient.

There is no world shortage of food. Europe has a 'set-aside' policy where farmers are paid not to grow food; we have butter-mountains and milk-lakes, and farmers drive unwanted sheep into town. India, with a high proportion of the hungry, exports grain and meat in huge quantities to wealthy countries. It is not lack of food but poverty, in an increasingly wealthy and unequal world, that condemns a billion people to live daily with the horror that they and their families may not have enough to eat.

The twenty companies that dominate the food trade would like us to believe that increasingly specialised crops, more sophisticated chemicals, genetic engineering and more globalisation are necessary to feed the world, i.e. more of the same. But modern food trade not only fails the hungry, it puts future production at risk.

Risk from chemical farming

7.5% of all arable land is abandoned every decade, largely because modern farming methods destroy the microorganisms that enrich the soil. Climate change will put many crops at risk, and the farming industry through its use of fossil fuel is a major cause. Dependence on chemicals puts poor farmers in debt, which cannot be repaid if a crop fails so, rather than just tightening their belts for a year, they lose their livelihood. Chemicals seep into ground water, putting drinking water at risk. Synthetic persistent organic compounds (POPs) are working up the food chain, endangering human and animal health. Spraying crops with chemicals upsets the balance of the natural predators which prevent individual insect populations getting out of hand; and insects develop resistance. The short-term advantage of insecticides soon turns into a long-term hazard.

Risk from monoculture

Biodiversity is fundamental to all life, so the current use of only the highest yield crops, a tendency towards monoculture, is contrary to sound science. During the 20th century three-quarters of the genetic diversity of agricultural crops was lost, and the rate of loss is increasing. 100,000 varieties of rice have been reduced to a few dozen and three-quarters of the world's rice now descends from a single plant. The prospect of climate change suggests that maximum diversity is more than ever desirable. The Irish experience with potatoes is only one warning out of many that monoculture is the herald of starvation.

FACT In India and China the number of suicides among farmers is now described as an epidemic. The cause is cheap imports, loss of land through debt and degradation of soil by chemicals.

Risk from specialisation

Crops are increasingly produced where they can be grown cheaply, and then transported around the world. This creates single-crop farming which makes the whole crop vulnerable. And the lower cost of mass production undermines the livelihood of local farmers in the receiving area. Having persuaded local farmers to grow a cash crop for export, the global company may suddenly drop them in favour of cheaper produce from elsewhere.

When societies become dependent on supplies from abroad, having lost their own local growers, the security of their food supply is put at risk.

🍎 Britain imports apples and, as a result, has lost most of its orchards

🍎 European dairy products are destroying local production in milk-rich Mongolia

🍎 Dutch butter costs less than Kenyan butter in the shops of Nairobi

🍎 Cheap wheat, subsidised by the US, is bankrupting thousands of Third World farmers .

Avoid risk

A secure future for food can be achieved if we use our present surplus to abandon industrial agriculture and establish sustainable local mixed farming methods.

FACT Keeping thousands of animals in close proximity allows viral infections to play havoc.

FACT The tendency to eat more meat is not sustainable: three hectares can produce either one tonne of beef, or between 50 and 100 tonnes of grains, pulses and vegetables. Half the European grain crop is used to feed livestock.

FACT International trade in grain has a risky future. The world's export capacity for grain is 200 million tonnes. The CIA estimates that China alone will need to import 200 million tonnes of grain in thirty years time.

The Earth Transformed
Gaudie and Vines
Blackwell 1997
ISBN 0 631 19465 7

Farming

has it gone mad?

For the consumer, farming has produced miracles. From the shelves of a supermarket we pick products from around the world, regardless of the seasons, and at lower prices than ever before. But, if we accept that we have a serious problem with pollution by fossil fuels, can this continue?

In Norfolk, tasteless but 'reliable' varieties of brussels sprouts are harvested with incredible wastage, taken to be packed in the Midlands, sent to a factory where they are washed, cleaned and sorted by size, packaged or frozen and then driven in refrigerated lorries back to Norfolk and sold, wrapped in cellophane, from cooled shelves.

More and more of what we pay for our food goes on inefficient mechanical methods, transport, storage, refrigeration, processing, packaging, administration and advertising. Often less than 20% of the cost goes to farmers - and much of

their income goes straight to suppliers of machinery and chemicals, or to the banks because of debt. Farmers have the highest incidence of clinical stress and suicide - no wonder small and medium-sized farms are becoming rarer by the year.

Farmers are paid subsidies. But they are paid at a flat rate per acre, so they need a large area. To be successful, industrial farmers need good administration, few workers, monoculture, high chemical input, and a contract to distribute their bulk produce around the country. In 1997 the E.U. gave intensive agribusiness $50 billion, and spent only $1 billion to encourage environmentally friendly farming.

But the consumer gets what she wants - or does she? Food poisoning in the UK has increased steadily from 14,000 cases in 1982 to 84,000 cases in 1998. With traditional mixed farming you might have bought some mud with your carrots, but it was safer than modern, sterilized, centralised food-distribution methods. These require more and more regulations which, in turn, make life difficult for small local shops, for local markets and for mixed farmers. Regulations and economies of scale require a centralised system - which creates more dangers. It is a self-perpetuating spiral of bureaucracy.

In order to avoid alarmist reporting there has been a lack of 'transparency' with research findings. So alarmist reporting is now rife, and the public is sceptical: being told, after years of cover-up, that we might be infected with mad cow disease; after dioxin deaths; after it was revealed that farmers didn't know what was in cattle feed; after it was revealed that meat products are used in jam and biscuits. Then the barbaric conditions for keeping battery chickens were only curbed after public pressure. Then there has been official resistance to labeling what is in our food. And when Dr Pusztai claimed that GM potatoes damaged the stomach lining of rats, he was immediately suspended and his research suppressed.

There must surely be a better way, such as:

• mixed farming that restores nutrients to the soil, thus requiring less use of chemicals;

• local distribution, so that people know where their food comes from: with less regulation and fewer lorries on the road;

• an economy that does not sink farmers into debt;

• 'public interest' research in place of 'corporate interest' research;

• research for farmers rather than for big companies; and research into sustainable farming methods.

• agriculture that sustains a rural community, that provides employment for people who enjoy working with plants and animals, that keeps our society in touch with its 'natural capital'.

Farming of this kind may be less efficient in achieving profits for highly organised business enterprises, but it is massively more productive per acre in real terms. It would bring the countryside to life, provide custom for local shops and transport, and make farming a modern, viable and satisfying occupation.

FACT 75% of food costs in the developed world lie in processing, packaging and distribution.

FACT In 50 years the US has, with intensive pesticide use, doubled the amount of crops lost to pests

FACT 80% of farm subsidy in the UK goes to the biggest and wealthiest 20% of farms.

FACT Daffodils from Cornwall go to Lincoln in refrigerated lorries, are flown to Holland for packaging, then flown back to the north of England, put onto another plane, and flown to New York for sale.

FACT British pig-farmers are now faced with swine fever. Last year 2,000 UK pig-farmers went out of business. 25 committed suicide.

FACT Cereal produced by industrial agriculture requires 6 or 7 times as much energy input as traditional mixed farming.

FACT In 1996 Britain exported 49 million kg of butter - and imported 47 million kg!

The Great Fruit Salad Story

Fruit salad from tree to table – a 'modern' fable.

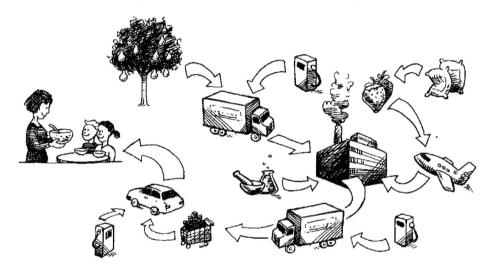

The Living Land
Jules Pretty
Earthscan 99
ISBN 1 85383 517 X

Organics

respecting nature's way

It is not just in retrospect that we can see the wrong turning that agriculture took last century. In 1896 Professor Shaler of Harvard University could say: "If mankind can't devise and enforce ways of dealing with the earth which will preserve the source of life, we must look forward to a time when our kind, having wasted its inheritance, will fade from the earth." Since then America has lost half its topsoil. It can take at least 500 years to develop an inch of topsoil, so the damage is immense.

Eve Balfour, one of the founders of the Soil Association, a woman in the man's world of mid-century agriculture, saw land as a fountain of energy flowing through a circuit of soils, plants and animals. She defined food chains as the living channels which conduct energy upwards, while death and decay return it to the soil. In 1946 she warned that chemicals like DDT would get into, and work their way up, the food chain; this is a hazard that took fifty years to enter the consciousness of administrators and it is only this year that the United Nations has put it among the top three global concerns.

Twenty years later Rachel Carson wrote 'The Silent Spring', which helped to start the ecology movement. It warned of a countryside depopulated, devoid of wildlife and devastated by chemicals. But since then, man's attack on nature has not been checked; it has intensified from minor skirmishes to all-out warfare as tractors compact the soil, herbicides destroy the humus, and pesticides kill micro-organisms, insects and natural predators. If agricultural scientists claim credit for improving the yield of specialised crops then they must also be held responsible for the tragic results of their myopic interventions. At last, at the opening of a new century, the general public is beginning to realise that our inheritance hangs in the balance.

When a farmer changes from chemical to organic farming, the productivity of his farm immediately drops. This is because the soil had been degraded by the chemicals. It takes several years to restore the land to full productivity. It is generally reckoned that the output of an organic farm will be less than a conventional farm, though a recent extensive study in the US found that the top quarter of sustainable mixed farms now have better yields than the top quarter of conventional farms. But organic farming has other 'yields'.

Eve Balfour linked the land with our mental, social and spiritual experience. She insisted that contact between town and country should be encouraged on every occasion, and that farming should be an integral aspect of education. It will be many years before this vision of truly organic sustenance can become a reality in the UK. It bears very little resemblance to 'supermarket organic' which uses planes and lorries to move produce around world, so cannot 'link' society with the soil. Yet the present interest in 'organic' produce is highly desirable and may yet cause us to change other aspects of our lives, too.

However, despite consumer enthusiasm, at 3%, the percentage of organic farms in the UK is among the lowest in Europe and conversion grants are half the European average. Meanwhile,11% of farmland in Austria is organic and conversion grants there are twice the European average.

FACT In Oxfordshire GM oilseed rape pollen was found three miles from a GM trial site. UK government rules require only a 50 metre separation. Organic farmers fear for their certification.

FACT 20% of insect species have, in the last 50 years, been lost in some parts of Britain. A quarter of our bee species faces extinction. Organic farming is the most cost effective way to restore biodiversity.

Living Earth
Magazine of the Soil Association
40 Victoria Street
Bristol, BS1 6BY

POP!

synthetic timebombs

In January 1999, in Belgium, transformer oil was accidentally mixed with fats destined for cattle feed. The oil contained two synthetic organic compounds, PCBs and furans, which are among the most toxic chemicals known. Ten feed manufacturers sold their products to 1,700 farmers in Belgium, who gave it to countless chickens, pigs, and cows.

Although the exposure in each mouthful of feed is minuscule, the contaminants concentrate in animal fat to much higher levels. By March PCBs and furans were found in chickens and eggs, several times the legal safe limit. By the end of May, retailers throughout Belgium dumped all poultry and egg products, including mayonnaise, cakes, and biscuits; farms slaughtered any animals suspected of carrying the poisons; and governments throughout the world banned importation of all Belgian animal products. Bad though this was for Belgium, it is only the tip of an iceberg worldwide.

POPs (persistent organic pollutants) are a legacy of the agrochemical revolution. They have been used since 1920 to kill pests, raise levels of food production and protect human health; they nearly eradicated malaria in tropical countries; and they are among the most important ingredients of modern industrial chemistry. They provided such widespread benefits that anyone questioning their use was accused of obstructing agricultural and industrial progress, and depriving the poor of protection against disease.

But POPs are toxic. They are persistent, man-made substances, not found in nature - therefore they offend one of the key principles of sustainability. They are now being found everywhere, from Europe to the Antarctic; and they are working their way up the food chain, from gulls and fish to seals and eagles. They accumulate and concentrate, so that we all now have 500 man-made organic chemicals in our bodies - mothers have many, including dioxin, in their breast milk.

POPs are associated with problems of the immune system; with delayed intellectual development; with reproductive problems; and with cancers. The United Nations, with 'unprecedented urgency', is trying to understand the problem, and wishes to phase out the use of POPs altogether, against strong opposition from industry and the US government.

POPs have joined the other major environmental hazards: they are synthetic time bombs.

But there is a related problem. The amount of pharmaceutical drugs entering the environment rivals the amount of pesticides. Traces of drugs used, from hormones and contraceptives to chemotherapy and fungicides, are found in plants, animals, fish and our drinking water. It is expected that the number of 'targets' for drugs will multiply twenty-fold following genome research. We cannot predict what the outcome of polluting the environment with drugs will be; it may be our biggest chemical challenge. Another synthetic time bomb is ticking.

FACT All products sold in Sweden in five years' time must be free of substances that are persistent and liable to accumulate, whether or not they are known to cause damage. The UK should follow their lead.

FACT More than 75,000 synthetic chemicals are now on the market. Nothing is known about a third of pesticides in common use, and only 10% have been properly tested.

FACT Scientists do not know how many POPs exist; there may be hundreds, but here is a dirty dozen:
(date introduced, use, and amount in million tons)

Dioxins: 1920s, herbicide, byproduct of combustion of treated wood and plastics, chlorine products and paper bleaching, (a constituent of Agent Orange used by the US to defoliate Vietnam)
Furans (dibenzofurans): 1920s, byproduct of PCBs and others
PCBs: 1929, refrigerants, foam insulation, aerosol propellants, cleaning solvents, adhesives. 1-2 mt
DDT: 1942, insecticide. 3mt
Hexachloro-benzine: 1945, fungicide and pesticide. 1-2 mt
Chlorodane: 1945, insecticide. 0.07 mt
Toxaphene: 1948, insecticide. 1.4 mt
Aldrin: 1949, insecticide. 0.24 mt
Dieldrin: 1948, insecticide. 0.24 mt
Heptachlor: 1948, insecticide.
Endrin: 1951, insecticide
Mirex: 1959, insecticide and fire retardant.

FACT In the last half century, the average sperm count of men throughout the world has halved.

FACT In 1940, a quarter of Americans could expect to contract cancer at some time in their lives. By 1990 the figure was 40% and rising. The WHO attributes 80% of cancer to environmental influence, so reducing chemical pollution would be five times as effective as finding expensive cures.

FACT First generation immigrants to the US have the low cancer incidence of their native land. Third generation immigrants have the high cancer incidence of the US.

State of the World 2000
Earthscan Publications Ltd
ISBN 1 85383 680 X

The Agrochemical Revolution

was it a success?

As the tractors rolled across the Tanzanian savannah Gidam, who is, or was, a nomad, spoke about the bung'eda mound inhabited by his father's spirit . "When the mound is ploughed" he said "the dead man's spirit is lost. You don't know where your father has gone. My children won't know where their grandfather is. We can no longer belong to this land". To agribusiness this is superstition, but to the nomads it was more significant than their forcible eviction, beatings, fines, imprisonment, murder, loss of cattle - the destruction of their way of life that forced them into city slums.

In 1970 the Canadian International Development Agency had a plan for producing food on an enormous scale. New seeds (Canadian), massive machines (Canadian) and chemicals (Canadian) would transform unproductive land. The savannah was turned into prairie farms. This project was capital intensive (Tanzania had no money) and used little labour (which they had). Initially the land was productive, but much of the thin topsoil ran off and blocked waterholes, the fragile ecology was destroyed and flash floods arrived. Tanzania was left with a massive debt. But this story has a hopeful, if fragile, ending - as farms are being abandoned due to soil degradation the nomads are returning and coaxing the land back to support their herds.

In India, Gandhian activists and the governments of several States are redistributing land to small farmers who cannot afford to buy seed, insecticides and fertilisers. They are trying to bring soil, degraded by chemicals, back to fertility and use saved seed; hence there is interest in organic farming and a strong anti-GM movement. Traditional farming benefits from complementary harvests such as wild plants, herbs, frogs, fish and shrimps, and its diversity protects it against changing conditions.

The Agrochemical Revolution in India entailed a massive programme of big-dam construction, where canals cut across natural watercourses. And the government subsidy policy of free water encouraged farmers to use water carelessly and abandon traditional tanks. Excessive irrigation has lowered water tables, has brought salts to the surface and turned much fertile land into desert. The recent drought in northern India has strengthened a movement to bring tanks back into use. These are large square constructions, many of them ancient, found all over the sub-continent. By channeling rainwater into them during the monsoon they provide water through the dry season and replenish the aquifers. It is called 'rainwater harvesting'.

Nehru, in 1947, had said "dams are the temples of modern India", but by 1958 he was having second thoughts: "the idea of big" he said " is not a good outlook at all . . . . it is the small irrigation projects, the small industries and the small plants for electric power, which will change the face of the country". At least fifty million people have been displaced by dams in India; there is no spare land, so they drift into city slums. The 155-dam project on the Narmada river and its tributaries will displace another half million people and destroy fertile land. The World Bank kick-started the Narmada project long before any technical and social research had been done; when they were eventually done, the Bank pulled out!

In Indonesia in the late 1970s vast areas were planted with a single variety of rice. These crops, which were sprayed with pesticide, were devastated by a pest called the brown plant-hopper. In fields just a few metres away, where pesticides had not been used, the natural predators of the plant-hopper flourished and healthy rice continued to grow.

Over thousands of years, humans have gradually improved the variety, yield and nutritional value of crops. Then, since 1950, the Agrochemical Revolution (inappropriately known as the Green Revolution) made a dramatic though fragile increase in production and irrigation. It allowed the world population to increase exponentially. But it has left a legacy of degraded soil, drained aquifers, silting dams, reduced crop-diversity, depopulated countryside, dependence on specialised seed, food transported over great distances, loss of antibiotics, and chemical-resistant pests, bacteria and fungus. A few companies now want to take this further and change the genetic basis of the world's food supply for commercial gain.

Our food supply, more than any other human activity, is dependent on intimate interaction with nature, but the Agrochemical Revolution and industrial farming have destroyed this close contact. Industrial farming should now be abandoned. However our increased scientific knowledge could lead us out of this mess. Research needs to be widened, and applied as never before, to achieve a genuinely sustainable food supply while making the activity of farming satisfying, secure, and available to the maximum number of people.

FACT **The yield of GM soya is 6% less than normal soya. This is the first GM crop with which rigorous tests have been carried out over a number of years.**

FACT **75% of the genetic diversity of agricultural crops was lost in the last century.**

No Man's Land
George Monbiot
Macmillan 1994
ISBN 0 333 60163 7

Pests and Weeds

putting humanity at risk

We imagine that the security and nutritional value of our food supply would grow as scientific knowledge grows. The reverse is happening.

Bacillus thuringiensis (Bt) bacteria are invaluable natural pesticides for organic growers. The bacteria were discovered in Thuringia, Germany, in 1911 and have been available in commercial formulations for insect control since the 1930s. Bt have a number of strains, including one that is effective against Colorado beetle, but they have been used sparingly by organic farmers because over-use would enable insects to develop resistance.

Biotechnology companies soon realised the potential for implanting these bacteria into the genetic make-up of plants, enabling the plants to grow with an in-built insecticide. Now genetically modified corn, cotton, potatoes and other plants have been widely planted, each carrying Bt in every cell. However, the plants are only protected from some pests, and are still sprayed against aphids and some sap-sucking insects.

Some of these novel plants have failed to perform, others have sent hordes of insects into neighbouring farms, and insect resistance has spread to surrounding crops and weeds, destroying natural predators that are essential for traditional farming. Even the biotech companies now admit that insects will develop resistance to Bt within five to eight years. This does not concern them because they are confident that their in-house scientists will come up with alternatives. But it will have deprived organic growers of their only natural insecticide.

The herbicide 'Roundup' had been highly profitable for Monsanto but its patent was due to run out in 1999; so their marketing department came up with a three-pronged strategy to prolong its value to the company. First: corn, cotton and soya have been genetically modified to resist it, so these crops can be sprayed with Roundup while they are growing. They said that environmentalists should be happy because less of the herbicide is necessary if you don't have to kill all weeds before sowing the crop.

Secondly, Monsanto bought seed merchants around the world so that they could instruct them to sell the 'Roundup Ready' seed.

Thirdly, they required farmers, when buying the seed, to sign an undertaking: "not to save any crop produced from this seed for replanting ... not to use this seed or provide it to anyone for crop breeding, research or seed production ... if a herbicide containing the same active ingredient as Roundup Ultra herbicide (or one with a similar mode of action) is used over the top of Roundup Ready soybeans, the Grower agrees to use only the Roundup branded herbicide". The company is allowed to enter farms to check whether farmers are saving and replanting seed and a hotline was set up to encourage farmers to tell on their neighbours - hardly the way to build community relations.

In 1998, 457 farmers in North America were sued. In some cases Monsanto seed had been 'identified' because the farmer's crops had been cross-pollinated from a neighbour's fields. The strategy was remarkably successful and now, in parts of America, few non-conforming farmers can protect their growing crops from the drift of Roundup spray.

Environmentalists and many farmers are alarmed by these developments. Less herbicide may be used, but the process is more effective in destroying biodiversity, creating sterile soil, and eliminating natural predators.

The marketing of limited, highly engineered seed by a handful of dominant companies, together with an attack on diverse landrace seed-saving by farmers, is the ultimate move towards monoculture. Science in the hands of business is depriving the world of natural products, introducing genetically novel plants, making soil sterile and encouraging monoculture. This is putting humanity at extreme risk.

FACT Herbicide-resistant GM plants can cross-pollinate with wild plants to create 'superweeds'.

FACT Since GM crops were introduced in the US, farmers have been using more pesticides and herbicides, not less.

FACT "Monsanto's 'New Leaf' potato incorporates pesticides in every cell, and the potato itself has to be registered as a pesticide.

> I, the fiery light of divine wisdom,
> I ignite the beauty of the plains,
> I sparkle the waters.
> I burn the sun and the moon and the stars,
> With wisdom I order all rightly.
> I adorn all the earth.
> I am the breeze that nurtures all things green.
> I am the rain coming from the dew
> That causes the grasses to laugh
> With the joy of life.
> I call forth tears, the aroma of holy work.
> I am the yearning for good.
>
> *Hildegard of Bingen*
> *1098 - 1179*

Genetic Engineering, Food,
and our Environment
Luke Anderson
Green Books 1999
ISBN 1 870098 78 1

Controlling the Food Chain

the terminator

The people we are talking about in this chapter are probably decent family men; they probably go to church and believe in a loving God; they probably follow normal business practice. So why are they feared?

'Terminator' technology was a logical business solution. Rather than paying lawyers to sue farmers for saving and sowing patented seed (see previous chapter), the seed could be genetically designed to commit suicide. This reduced its yield slightly, and did not exactly improve humanity's ability to cultivate, but Monsanto's friends in the United States Department of Agriculture (USDA) were happy to help. Let's just quote them.

Monsanto: "Terminator technology will open significant world-wide seed markets to the sale of transgenic technology, for crops in which seed currently is saved and used in subsequent plantings."

US government spokesman, Willard Phelps: "terminator technology's primary function is to increase the value of proprietary seed owned by US seed companies and to open up new markets in second and third world countries".

Melvin J Oliver, USDA scientist, not a company man, explains: "Our mission is to protect US agriculture and to make us competitive in the face of foreign competition. Without this there is no way of protecting the patented seed technology".

Recently, due to intense anger world-wide, Monsanto agreed to delay marketing terminator seed for further studies on environmental, economic and social effects. They grudgingly admitted that "we need some level of public acceptance to do our business".

Other companies are also turning plant welfare on its head for commercial gain.

- AstraZeneca is developing seed that is sterile unless their own chemicals are applied.

- Novartis is even developing plants whose resistance to viruses and bacteria have been removed.

Plants that are sterile, plants that die without chemicals, plants that have no resistance to disease – these are among the achievements of biotechnology companies. And they claim that patents on life forms are necessary to enable them to invest in this research.

But that is not all; controlling humanity's food source is only a part of Monsanto's ambitions. To quote Bob Shapiro, Chief Executive: "It is truly easy to make a great deal of money dealing with primary needs: food, shelter, clothing."

"What you are seeing" said Robert Farley of Monsanto in 1998 after describing their purchase of seed companies throughout the world "is not just a consolidation of seed companies, it's really a consolidation of the entire food chain. Since water is as central to food production as seed is, Monsanto is now trying to establish its control over water. Monsanto plans to launch a new water business, starting with India and Mexico, since both these countries are facing water shortages. These are the markets that are most relevant to us as a life science company committed to delivering food, health and hope to the world, and in which there are opportunities to create business value".

Monsanto Strategy Paper: "We are enthusiastic about the potential of partnering the World Bank in joint venture projects in developing markets. The Bank is eager to work with Monsanto."

Many Indians understand this to mean that Monsanto aims to control the vital resources of the Indian sub-continent, using public finances (the World Bank) to underwrite the investment. Indian agriculture would then be at the mercy of a private company motivated by profit.

By 2025 in India the need for water will be fifty percent more than will be available. The crisis will be even greater if the Himalayan glaciers, which supply summer water to the Indus and the Ganges, continue to shrink. It is predicted that the glaciers will be gone in 35 years. The water table in most states in India is dropping one metre a year. Water companies will be more interested in industry than in poor farmers and thirsty peasants.

FACT **Commercial Funding of Research**

Most research is now funded by commercial organisations. Even government bodies are dominated by commercial interests. Universities look for projects that will attract commercial funding and researchers publicise results that are acceptable to their funders.

The first peer-reviewed study of the effects of commercial funding, in 1998, confirmed that researchers are indeed influenced. The study related to concern over whether calcium-channel-blockers, used for treating high blood pressure, might increase the risk of death. Researchers examined seventy authors of articles on both sides of the controversy. Among supporters of the drug all except two had financial relations with manufacturers of calcium-channel-blockers, and even those two had funding from the drugs industry.

The message is clear: it is naïve to expect impartial statements from people whose careers are tied to the development of a technology. Few scientists will not allow funding to influence their opinion.

Microbes

tougher than humans?

Human beings may be clever, but the humble microbe will outlive us.

Let's start with the big picture. It took four billion years for living cells to transform the virgin soup of the atmosphere - a toxic, chaotic mixture of methane, sulfurous compounds, carbon dioxide, and other substances - into conditions that could support life. We must thank the microbes for creating quality out of chaos. In the last few decades we, in our wisdom, started to reverse all this. We are digging up everything the microbes 'fixed', we are creating novel materials and gases and disgorging them into the sky and onto the earth's crust. Earth is now running backwards into the chaotic garbage heap from which it started.

But the microbes are still at work. Bacteria, viruses, protozoa, yeasts and algae live in the soil, in water, in the air, on our skin, in our bodies, and are key players in maintaining suitable conditions for life. They recycle nutrients for plants, and in our gut they provide vitamins and aid digestion. And, though we can't see them, we use them to make wine, bread, cheese and yoghurt.

Microbes have awesome power. A single bacterium can, given the right conditions, take less than a day to multiply to a thousand billion cells. So a policy of understanding and cooperation, as practised in organic farming and in much eastern medicine, might be more enlightened than zapping them whenever they harm our crops or cause us pain.

Our close contact with domestic animals at the dawn of civilization allowed microbes to jump from them to us, originating many of our 'crowd' diseases: smallpox and tuberculosis came from cattle, the common cold from horses. We developed partial immunity through long contact, but Polynesians and native Americans had virtually no defense when they first came into contact with Europeans carrying these diseases. Pigs have had a bad record more recently: they were responsible for the Asian 'flu' epidemic of 1918-20 which killed 20 million people, more than were killed in the Great War and, in April 1999, seventy Malaysians died from a virus contracted from pigs. This may be a cause for caution over xenotransplantation, where pigs are used for growing human spare parts. We are now coming into close contact with a host of unfamiliar microbes as virgin forests are being felled. It is now widely accepted that the AIDS epidemic started through experiments by an American biotech company with a vaccine derived from chimpanzee kidneys. Other infections are expected to jump when their natural hosts deplete. Natural immunity takes a long time to evolve.

In the 1960s many doctors believed that infectious diseases would soon be conquered, but this hope is now fading and medicine is increasingly seen as a race to keep ahead of pathogenic microbes. As soon as cures or new drugs are found, resistant bacteria seem to develop. Many hospitals have had to close wards due to untreatable bacteria or viruses, particularly MRSA. Malaria is spreading north from the tropics. Tuberculosis, which was thought to have been beaten, is coming back, and some strains are already untreatable - so that, in New York, the medieval practice of forcible isolation has been reintroduced. In the US the West Nile virus is now causing massive panic, so that everything in sight gets sprayed.

Human presence is the flicker of an eyelid in the timetable of microbes. We cannot assume that humans are somehow above the evolutionary battle and are bound to survive whatever damage we do to other forms of life on earth. A little less arrogance would serve us well.

It's not all bad news. SmithKline Beecham is providing billions of free doses of albendazole in an effort to wipe out elephantiasis, a horrible disease, over the next 20 years - a huge act of corporate philanthropy.

The Conquest of Disease
Understanding Global Issues 98/2
ISBN 0 85048 704 8

Superbugs and Antibiotics

a gift of nature rejected

In just sixty years we have thrown away the advantages of a modern medical miracle.

The first of the five 'kingdoms of life' on earth consisted of bacteria. Some of these are also known as germs because they can invade the human body and cause disease. Bacterial infection, however, can be treated by antibiotics, and the first, penicillin, became available in the 1940s – a medical miracle. There are now fifteen types of antibiotic, though more may be developed, each of which acts in a different way.

High doses of antibiotic kill bacteria. But when bacteria are subject to low-level doses, some survive and some die. The ones that survive have a reproductive advantage. By this process the bacteria develop immunity relatively quickly. This is why doctors only prescribe antibiotics when necessary and insist that you complete the course. Modern surgery was not possible until 1945 when penicillin could kill the most infectious agent, Staphylococcus Aureus (SA). By 1947 some SA had become resistant to penicillin. In 1957 methicillin was introduced and methicillin-resistant-SA bacteria (MRSA) developed within two years, making the wards of some hospitals unusable. Now only Vancomysin controls MRSA's worst excesses, but for how long? Vancomysin-resistant bugs have already been detected. Within a few years SA may again become untreatable. A cut finger could be fatal.

Like humans, animals that are kept in unnatural and crowded conditions are, particularly susceptible to disease. So what do farmers do? They feed their animals regular doses of antibiotics! The appalling condition of battery chickens is well known, but systematic cruelty and overcrowding are common with many forms of animal husbandry. So we should not be surprised that resistant bacteria develop in these conditions and go on to affect humans; one's only surprise is that the experts are surprised. It has taken till now for Britain's government to admit: "We believe that the evidence shows conclusively that giving antibiotics to animals results in the emergence of some resistant bacteria which infect humans". Fish farming also uses antibiotic prophylactics.

What sort of society are we that it is only fear for our own health that has made us take any interest in providing healthy and humane conditions for animals?

You may think that plants do not carry antibiotics, but they now do. Most genetically modified (GM) crops, which have been planted all over the American mid-west and on test sites in Europe, carry antibiotic genes. Bacteria must be jumping for joy because this low-level presence will allow them to develop resistance.

Why has there been so little control over the use of antibiotics in agriculture? It is only a question of time before 'superbugs' will result from the routine use of antibiotic prophylactics in animal feed and from the implantation, of antibiotic 'marker' genes in GM crops. When this happens we face the prospect of **untreatable epidemics sweeping the world**. Will the first pandemic arise from the chicken batteries of Europe or from the genetically modified plains of mid-west America?

FACT 60% of infections picked up in hospitals are now drug-resistant. The World Health Organisation (WHO) says that it is a question of time before microbes become resistant to the last effective antibiotic.

Against the Grain
Marc Lappé and Britt Bailey
Earthscan 1999
ISBN 1 85383 576 5

Genes

and genetic experimentation

Don't skip this page just because it's complex stuff! Genes are important, too important to be left to scientists.

Genes are units of heredity - they reproduce themselves from one generation to another. They are fragments of the DNA sequence which have cohesive ends enabling them to be extracted and recombined, hence genetic experimentation is often referred to as "recombinant DNA" technology. How are genes transferred from one organism to another? Strangely, by infection. Modified strains of viruses and bacteria - particularly E.coli - have been used as vectors since the 1970s in the US. These new strains have to be particularly powerful in order to infect totally unrelated organisms. The transferred gene cannot be placed with accuracy so an antibiotic 'marker' gene is attached to identify where it ends up. The new organism thus carries low-level antibiotics. It is a haphazard process so 'genetic engineering' is a misnomer; one should be talking about 'genetic experimentation'.

The science is in its infancy - at the stage of dropping toys out of the cot to see if they break. But it is an immensely exciting game for molecular biologists as they are creating life forms which have never existed in nature before, by combining genes across species, across genera, and across kingdom boundaries. For example, a potato may now carry the gene that stops a fish freezing.

But new forms of life may carry new, uncontrollable, dangers. James Watson, joint discoverer of DNA, issued, with other scientists, an alarming open letter in 1974. Genetic experiments will "result in the creation of novel types of infectious DNA elements" they said "whose biological properties cannot be completely predicted in advance . . . new DNA elements introduced into E.coli might possibly become widely disseminated among human, bacterial, plant, or animal populations with unpredictable effects". They called for a moratorium on high-risk recombinant DNA experiments. But within a year the potential financial profits from genetic experimentation became irresistible and many scientists were hooked. In Scotland and Japan, as Watson predicted, there have been incidents where modified E.coli has escaped the laboratory with disastrous results. Dr Ho goes as far as to suggest that this technology could be the end of humanity. Dare we ignore her?

Scientists have found the DNA sequences of nearly all the genes on all 23 pairs of chromosomes found in every human cell. This is a staggering achievement, but it could be compared to a chef finding the Roux brothers' larder but not the genius of their cooking.

Everyone has between 30,000 and and 120,000 genes; scientists are still undecided which figure is closer. Computers can cope with this. But the human body is made up of cells and an adult has about a hundred thousand billion cells; most cells have a complete set of the genes. The genes turn themselves on or off in different ways in different cells according to their environment, in what has been described as a symphony of gene expression; this may explain why chimpanzees, which share 98.5% of our genes, are different from us in almost every detail. Scientists are also undecided whether a genetic disorder is due to the malfunction of a gene, protein, chromosome or cell.

Changing the genes in every cell of an organism is massively complex. But to modify the egg and sperm before genes divide is relatively simple because you are only changing a single cell; this is called germ-line therapy. This modified gene will reproduce itself in every cell of the organism as it grows, and will be present in future generations - germ-line therapy is in effect artificial evolution. Germ-line experiments have been successfully carried out on mammals, and researchers expect the first human trials to be conducted within the next few years.

We should, in humility, question whether we will ever fully understand life, and where our experiments with genes will lead. History is full of our mistakes. But mistakes with life will have a life of their own.

FACT E.coli is normally harmless. The deadly E.coli 0157:H7 first appeared in the US in 1982. 9,000 people were affected in Japan in 1992. Last year there were 1,084 cases in the UK.

FACT Vitamin A can be inserted into GM rice to prevent blindness. Scientists have pointed out that many crops have this property and medicine could easily be distributed; so there is no need to introduce the risks that GM technology pose for poor farmers.

Genetic Engineering
Dr Mae-Wan Ho
Gateway Books 1998
ISBN 1 85860 052 9

Nature in Balance

survival of the fittest?

The skeletal structure of the Oxford Museum, with a giant dinosaur across its main hall, is where the first debates on the origin of species took place. In a cabinet there are two bean-weevils which are so small they can sit comfortably on a match head, but their rate of reproduction is prodigious. Beside them is a glass jar. Dr George McGavin, the curator, says that it would take only about seventy days of unchecked mating of the weevils and their progeny for the jar to be filled with their eggs. If they continued thus they would fill the iguanadon in a hundred days and the entire internal volume of the Earth in a little over fifteen months. If this happened they would, of course, have nothing to eat. By winning, they would be on the losing side. Nature, during four billion years, has evolved plenty of checks to stop this happening. If any species is too successful its population may suddenly collapse.

Each species needs a balanced habitat to provide it with food, and each species is subject to a balance of predators and microbes. But the balance can be rocked. When a plant or creature from one part of the world is introduced into another it may no longer have the natural restraints that had evolved in its original habitat. Biologists refer to the ten/ten principle: one in ten alien organisms will thrive in a new environment and one in ten of those that thrive will become a pest.

There were no rabbits in Australia until a few were deliberately introduced in 1859; they soon spread throughout the continent with disastrous effects. A single Japanese Knotweed, planted in a garden near Brighton, escaped into a rubbish tip and has now spread throughout the UK. It is unaffected by pesticides. Swansea has a full-time Knotweed officer and he reckons it would cost £10 million to eradicate it from the city - it would return, of course. Mink escaping from farms in the UK have threatened the survival of some native species. The grey squirrel has displaced the red squirrel in England. The zebra mussel has caused havoc in the Great Lakes of North America. The comb jellyfish has colonized the Black Sea. Water hyacinth has clogged waterways in Africa and India.

Whether the 10/10 principle will apply to genetically modified plants and animals is an open question. Some novel organisms are being deliberately released as trial crops. In laboratories, novel bacteria and viruses are developed as vectors to transfer genes from one species to another. Animals with altered genes are being introduced into agriculture and human surgery. But once novel plants, bacteria, viruses or animals are out in the open they have a life of their own and they are no longer in our control. As they are new to nature it is unlikely they will be subject to the constraints that have developed over millions of years.

Seen from space the biosphere seems a fragile skin, as delicate as the bloom on a peach. But humanity is infinitely more fragile. We do not control nature, nature supports us. Nature has evolved in a way that retains a balance. The forests act as the lungs of the world and contain unexplored genetic richness; plants and plankton begin the food chain on land and sea; microorganisms make the soil fertile and enable creatures to digest food - but it is presumptuous to comment on this infinite complexity. Creatures that disturb this balance find themselves rejected.

Where Next
Duncan Poore
Manor Group 2000
ISBN 1 84246 000 5

Population

more or less

The world population in 2050 will be decided by three billion women. If every second woman decides to have three rather than two children, the population will be 27 billion. The best guess is that, on average, women will have 2.1 children, the 'fertility rate', and the population will increase from 6 billion now to 10.8 billion. If, however, every second woman decides to have only one child instead of two, the world population will sink to 3.6 billion. Tiny changes in people's motivation result in huge changes to numbers, so there is a case for being sceptical about predictions. Many assumptions are made about people's motivation in deciding to have, or not to have, children and obviously many forms of pressure and health aspects play their part. Education and health, for example, can be the most effective vehicles for reducing the growth of population. But demographers are also under pressure from politicians who like to hear that economic growth will restrain population, and from corporations who can use the scare of rising numbers to justify risky experiments with chemicals and genes.

Stable societies in the past, to some extent, had an understanding of 'carrying capacity' – the ability of their environment to sustain the desired quality of life over a long period. For example, the early colonisers of America had significantly larger families than their close relatives in crowded Europe. But improved agriculture and the technical aid programmes of the 20th century released families particularly in the South from this bondage and they felt confident in having more children, hence the population explosion. We face the paradox that the expectation of food security increased population but the number of hungry people is now greater than at any time in world history.

Human population increased very gradually over hundreds of thousands of years. Then, following the industrial revolution, the rate of growth suddenly increased, particularly since 1950. But since the 1970s there has been a gradual reduction in the rate of growth in most parts of the world. The usual way of predicting numbers is to guess at fertility rates and assume that, since they have always increased in the past, they will continue to increase, though the recent slow-down will lead to a ceiling figure in due course.

But demographers also use the technique of fitting a mathematical equation to past trends. This has been done and shows a startlingly different outcome. The graph levels off in twenty years' time and then drops rapidly to pre-industrial levels. Demographers who favour the mathematical method point out that it is based on fact whereas the official approach is based purely on conjecture. The reducing populations of Italy and Russia may be the beginning of this trend. The burden of proof is therefore on those who predict continuing growth.

The mathematical approach presents a serious warning because it has affinity with current developments. Our plentiful supply of cheap energy is declining; low-lying cities may be flooded and agriculture threatened due to climate-change; ice-age aquifers are being exhausted; the 'natural capital' of the world is reducing; past diseases return and new ones appear; ethnic conflict is increasing - all point to a higher mortality rate. These tendencies, together with an ageing population and falling confidence in western culture, could provide feedback that reduces parents' perception of their future prospects, thus reducing the fertility rate. A reduced fertility rate and increased mortality could be the mechanism by which the mathematical prediction is confirmed.

So the surge of population during the last century may be a temporary phenomenon brought on by access to the cheap energy on which almost all our technology depends. In due course the human population may return to a level that is within the carrying capacity of the world.

Population Politics
Virginia Abernethy
Transaction 1999
ISBN 0 765806 037

Patenting Life

wait a minute! Who made it?

Only 'commerce' could think of 'privatising' life forms. An African tribal-doctor might wish to keep his remedies secret but no one would deny others the chance to emulate him. Indians know trees by their medicinal properties, and the idea that anyone should pay a fee for using these properties is inconceivable. It has been axiomatic that anyone in the world can use the resources of nature - until twenty years ago.

It happened in th US. A genetically engineered microorganism, designed to consume oil spills, provided the test case. The Patents and Trademark Office (PTO) rightly rejected the application, arguing that living things could not be patented under US law. But at appeal the patent was allowed by a narrow majority on the basis that the microorganism was "more akin to inanimate chemical compositions than to horses and honeybees". The PTO, still believing that patenting life forms was wrong, appealed to the Supreme Court, which upheld the patent in 1980. But four of the nine judges strongly opposed it and it was nearly rejected.

Then in 1987 the PTO did an astonishing about-turn. It issued a ruling that all genetically engineered living organisms can be patented - including human genes, cell-lines, tissues, organs, and even genetically altered human embryos and foetuses. This ruling opened the flood gates.

Patented things have to be 'novel, non-obvious and useful'. No one has ever argued that oxygen or helium, for example, however non-obvious and however useful, can be patented just because a chemist has isolated, classified, and described their properties. These elements are not novel;

they exist in nature. But with total lack of consistency the PTO now holds that anyone can claim a human invention simply by isolating and classifying a gene's properties and purposes, even though these are not novel, but pre-exist in nature. No molecular biologist has ever created a gene, cell, tissue, organ, or organism *de novo*.

The first mammal to be patented was a mouse with human genes. The team that created Dolly the sheep applied for a broad patent to cover all cloned animals. Then, a businessman, John Moore, received hospital treatment for a rare form of cancer; later he found that the University of Los Angeles had patented his body parts and licenced them to a pharmaceutical company at a value of $3 billion; the California Supreme Court ruled that Moore had no rights over his own body tissues. A broad patent gives Briocyte worldwide ownership of all human blood cells from the umbilical cord of babies, for pharmaceutical purposes, even though the company has only isolated and described the blood cells.

Broad patents have caused furore. Patenting of the properties of the Neem tree and Basmati rice by American companies has provoked violent anger throughout India. An American professor failed in his attempt to patent turmeric for medicinal purposes, but it cost India $500,000 to fight the case. Papua New Guinea was furious to discover that the US government had patented cell lines from its citizens. The arrogance of this new colonialism is breathtaking. Patents take no account of the transformation of wild grasses, tubers etc. into crops by indigenous people over millennia. They literally allow northern companies to hijack knowledge that has been used by all – even nature itself – and charge others for using it. But poor nations fear sanctions if they do not adopt American practice on patenting.

The World took a wrong turning in America twenty-three years ago. It seems unlikely that the UK government will put principle above commercialism. But India might declare, unilaterally, that the fundamental elements of life are global commons and ought never to be up for sale to private interests at any price. All life knowledge, at present in private hands, would then be freely available on the sub-continent. Perhaps India would become the power-house of the life-sciences because of this free availability of knowledge.

Commercial Eugenics

will life science lead us by the nose?

Economic inequality has become extreme. But redistribution of wealth is extremely unpopular among the rich who wield power. They may decide to 'solve' humanity's biggest problem by taking inequality into new spheres

Our mental capacity evolved to meet the needs of hunter-gatherers and is built into our genes. Even the most primitive tribal, given the right training, can use the internet. So, by imagining hunter-gatherer society, some believe, we can begin to understand some human oddities - man is promiscuous and woman coy because that helps his genes to multiply and hers to use their annual chance to obtain quality. It is a compulsive game that you can play according to your interests.

A *sociologist* asks why we are able to co-operate well in groups up to 150 but are often hopeless at larger scale decision-making. *An art historian* asks why we like landscape paintings that have an edge-of-forest feel. Evolutionary psychology is a surprisingly static cause-and-effect type of theory.

Scientists have latched onto the popular cause-and-effect concept because it captures the imagination and helps to release funds. Almost daily scientists claim to find genes for this and that: a gene for inherited disease, for alcoholism, for aggression, for depression, for dyslexia...

Finding and neutralising the gene for Down's Syndrome would be one of the great achievements of medicine. If air traffic controllers could be screened for genetic predisposition to black out it would surely be our duty to protect the public. If we could find correlation between a gene and aggressive behaviour perhaps we could reduce crime - in California genetic scans are already used in the sentencing process to determine whether a convicted criminal is likely to re-offend.

Then insurance companies are bound to ask for genetic screening or at least for us to declare any tests that show genetic pre-dispositions. Employers will want to check that their investment in trainees is unlikely to be wasted. The billionaire will want to ensure that his progeny are tall, intelligent and sociable - all traits which, it is claimed, can be enhanced by genetic modification. We are at an early stage of the science, but if these techniques become possible they are bound to be adopted.

Instead of having a genetic make-up that was developed for hunter-gatherers and is ill adapted to modern society, **we can now change our genes to suit our present needs**. In our market-driven society this will no doubt be achieved through personal and commercial incentive.

Molecular Biologist Lee Silver of Princetown University regards himself as one of the scientists blazing a trail to a future containing the Gene-Rich and the Naturals. The Gene-Rich, offspring of today's super-rich, will be about 10% of the population, enhanced with synthetic genes and having the life-span of Methuselah. **The Gene-Rich will become the rulers of society** - businessmen, musicians, artists, athletes and scientists. "With the passage of time" Lee Silver predicts "the genetic distance will become greater and greater, and there will be little movement up from the Natural to the Gene Rich class. Naturals will work as low-paid service providers or as labourers" no doubt with good television to divert them. "Gene-Rich humans and Natural humans will be entirely separate species with no ability to cross-breed and with as much romantic interest in each other as a current human would have for a chimpanzee".

The higher species may treat us as we treat lesser species. A humane cull may be necessary to tackle our biggest problem - the adverse environmental effects of excessive numbers.

The Biotech Century
Jeremy Rifkin
Tarcher/Putnam 1998
ISBN 0 87477 953 7

Understanding Nature

and re-designing life

Our understanding of the world around us is determined, to a great extent, by the culture in which we live.

St Thomas Aquinas saw the natural world as a Great Chain, a myriad of plants and animals in a descending hierarchy of importance. For him nature required dependent relationships and obligations among creatures that God had created. Diversity and inequality guaranteed the orderly working of the system. His portrayal of nature reflected the hierarchical structure of medieval society in which he lived.

Later, Darwin's portrayal of nature also reflected the society in which he lived. The capitalist marketplace was competitive, where only the fittest survived, and his theories about plants, animals or man reflected this. As with men's development of machines, evolution in nature produced better and better models. His theory precisely matched Adam Smith's 'invisible hand' which enabled acts of individual selfishness to result in general well-being. The intrinsic value of each living thing in the medieval paradigm was replaced by mere 'utility' value.

Nowadays nature is being cast in the image of the computer and information science. Creatures are no longer birds and bees, foxes and hens, but bundles of genetic information with no sacred boundaries between species. In commerce, new groups of companies are emerging, having shared relationships within complex embedded networks which are able to respond quickly to fast-changing flows of information. A generation brought up in a computerised society can accept information as a basis for understanding nature. It reassures us that the infinite and chaotic complexities and multi-faceted expansions of all our activities, our ever-shifting life-styles, and our experimentation with genes, are in harmony with the evolutionary processes of nature. Thus we avoid feeling confused and threatened.

In the 1940s Norbert Wiener pioneered the concept that "all living things are really patterns that perpetuate themselves. A pattern is a message and may be transmitted as a message; the fact that we cannot telegraph the pattern of a man from one place to another seems to be due to technical difficulties", a concept that will be familiar to viewers of Star Trek.

The ability to handle information, rather than to develop knowledge or wisdom, is typical of modern life: today's understanding gives way to tomorrow's; we must be continually open to new scenarios; through drugs and plastic surgery we can reinvent ourselves; life and work are games to be played.

Molecular biologists no longer talk of laws of nature or objective reality, but of 'scenarios', 'models', 'creative possibilities' - this is the language of architects or artists. Those at the cutting edge see their ability to handle almost unlimited information through computers (soon to be living DNA computers) as a natural extension of evolution. Evolution has now passed into their hands (they say 'into humanity's hands' but who else has the ability except molecular biologists?). Molecular biologists are the artists of new forms of life; they will modify and design future generations. In other words they are the 'invisible hand' of Darwin's natural selection or the God of St. Thomas Aquinas.

Intuition

common sense, imagination, and morality

Science is largely responsible for our progress and prosperity, and it is natural to look first to scientists for the answers to difficult questions. A refrain of the present government is that "we will work to the best scientific advice".

But science, almost by definition, is 'reductionist' - it looks at the simple constituents of complex things. Science can improve crop yields but not get the additional food to hungry mouths. Scientists have made no secret of their ignorance about the political effects of nuclear energy, and these effects have proved more important than the science itself. Governments like to claim scientific support partly because it allows them to make decisions within a cabal of experts, bureaucrats and corporate managers, hidden from the public behind obscure language. But recent events suggest that we should give more weight to intuition, imagination, common sense and morality.

Intuition might have prevented us turning cows into cannibals - we would have avoided BSE, cattle would have suffered less, we would have saved £5 billion and we would have more friendly neighbours across the Channel.

Imagination could show that clear labeling of content and origin would enable epidemiologists to trace what is happening in a complex food system, and help people to make informed decisions on what they wish to buy.

Common sense would tell us that a centralised food system is dangerous - without such a system eight litres of transformer oil would not have destroyed Belgium's entire food economy in

1999. Common sense surely tells us that field-testing crops that are genetically new to nature, on the basis of 'lets see what happens', could be rather like releasing rats to see whether or not they spread bubonic plague. Common sense tells us that the cost of coal, oil, gas and water should reflect depletion and contribution to climate change, not just the cost of extraction.

Morality tells us not to keep chickens in such crowded conditions that they can't walk, live only six weeks and are then shackled upside down to a conveyor belt before being killed. If we had avoided this cruelty we would not now suffer from salmonella. Morality tells us to ban BST hormone treatment because it causes acute suffering to cows, let alone the suffering it might cause humans. Morality tells us not to participate in inhuman trading practices. Morality, eventually, told us to stop slavery.

When intuition, imagination, common sense or morality - let alone science - suggest that a new policy, product or procedure is suspect, it should be the responsibility of the promoter to prove that the objections are unfounded - this is the 'precautionary principle'. Our government and the World Trade Organisation act on the basis that no restriction must be allowed until conclusive evidence shows harm. By then the damage is done.

Some countries use citizen's juries, chosen at random, who are presented with some technical background and a host of expert and lay views as to whether a certain area of research is worth pursuing. After hearing the evidence, the citizen's jury come to a verdict as to whether the research seems reasonable and fair by criteria that they themselves develop. Both scientists and political theorists have been surprised and impressed by the results.

Captive State:
The Corporate Takeover of Britain
George Monbiot
Macmillan 2000
ISBN 0 330369 431

Two Japanese Farmers

more with less - a fascinating tale

Weeding rice paddy-fields is very labour intensive so Japanese farmers eagerly adopted the chemical approach, even though it did not improve on the high yield of traditional Japanese methods. Only a few farmers held back from the Agrochemical Revolution.

The Furunos are a Japanese farming couple who do not use chemicals. Their system uses ducklings to fertilise the fields and eat the weeds. The rice has a very high yield and they get four different harvests: rice, fish (roach), eggs and ducks. In spite of having spent their life perfecting the system they are happy for it to be adopted by anyone: "financial success is unimportant. We did not patent the method, we just want it to be widely adopted". 10,000 farmers now use the method in Japan and it is spreading throughout South-East Asia.

Masanobu Fukuoka inherited a farm from his father. He claims to be lazy. If things grow in the wild on their own, why does one have to do so much hard work? he would ask. So in a short time he had destroyed his father's orange orchard and was having similar success (sic!) with the rice. But he persisted with his unusual convictions and over the years developed a system of 'do nothing' farming. He does not flood his rice fields, he does not weed them, he does not dig or plough and above all he does not use any chemicals. Yet his crops are resistant to pests, yield as much as traditional or chemical rice growing, and require much less work.

But the system requires careful management of crops and is related to a particular location; the farmer needs to know the micro-climate and be observant. In the autumn he sows rice, clover and winter barley and covers them with straw. The barley grows immediately and is harvested in May and its straw scattered on the fields. The spring monsoon weakens the weeds and allows the rice to grow through the ground cover. Nothing more is done until the rice is harvested in October. Over the years the soil has got richer and richer with no ploughing, without taking away the straw, and with no addition of manure or fertilisers. "This is a balanced rice field ecosystem" he says "insect and plant communities maintain a stable relationship here. It is not uncommon for a plant disease to sweep through the area, leaving the crops in these fields unaffected".

He has a similar approach to his restored orchard, harvesting a great variety of vegetables under the trees without cultivation but with a lot of care. He has plenty of spare time to be a philosopher.

Both farmers achieve yields that could make Japan self-sufficient in food, but the government persists in supporting chemical methods using alien seed. "Because the world is moving with such furious energy in the opposite direction" Fukuoka-sen says "it may appear that I have fallen behind the times, but I firmly believe that the path I have been following is the most sensible one".

The One Straw Revolution
Masanobu Fukuoka
The Other India Press 1992
ISBN 81 85569-32-2

Mental Equipment

reality beyond our grasp

Our brains did not appear suddenly from nowhere, they evolved in the same way that other parts of our bodies evolved. Gradually, over hundreds of thousands of years, those with greater abilities supplanted others. Our mental equipment is therefore appropriate for specific needs, and is related to our five senses. It is not an abstract intelligence designed to comprehend all of existence, however much we use this equipment to understand and manipulate the world around us. It has limitations.

To appreciate the implications you only have to imagine a group that lacks one of the five senses, a group that has been blind from birth, discussing sight. They have heard people talk about colour, about clouds, about mist, about distance and about beauty. How would they discuss these concepts among themselves? Some might say it is all a myth and deny that sight exists; some might be acutely frustrated that they can't quite grasp the idea; some might develop a form of words and bully others to accept their definition; and others might be more tentative and try to feel their way into an understanding.

If our cognitive equipment evolved to meet the needs of hunter-gatherers, it is not surprising that some aspects of reality are simply beyond our grasp, just as a dog picks up only part of your meaning: 'blah blah blah fido blah blah'. But we do seem to sense further reality through a dark distorting glass. Our vague perceptions are the stuff of mystics, poets, musicians and painters. Religions have tried to tie these realities down into concepts and words.

Even scientists describe things that fall beyond comprehension. Newtonian physics and Cartesian geometry made sense to our five senses. No longer. Matter is now known to be a mass of energy, more like a web of interpenetrating vibrations than like solid building blocks; particles of energy are connected to each other in mysterious ways, seemingly unlimited by space and time; an experiment is changed by being viewed. Scientists now even suggest that 'string', with ten dimensions and a whole world of magnitude below the size of molecules, could give clues for understanding the universe. All this points to connections at a far deeper level than we can fully comprehend.

If there were creatures whose cognitive equipment had evolved beyond ours, they might be amused at the way we describe concepts that are mysterious to us but clear and obvious to them. But they might also be alarmed that our technology allows us to play with things whose full interconnectedness we can't possibly appreciate – they might see us wandering towards the precipice and be shouting 'for God's sake STOP!'

"Failing to understand the consequences of our inventions... seems to be a common fault of scientists and technologists. We are being propelled into the new century with no plan, no control and no brake."
Bill Joy.
Chief Scientist, Sun Microsystems

How the Mind Works
Stephen Pinker
Allen Lane 1997
ISBN 0 713 991305

Some Conclusions

by Alastair Sawday, the publisher

"Technology is the answer". Really? What was the question?

A classic error of western 'civilisation' has been to deal with, say, the energy crisis, by asking "How can we generate more electricity?", rather than "How can we generate the minimum amount of electricity to meet our needs without damaging the environment?"

The same people are allowed to provide both question and solution.

Environmentalists are nevertheless excited about the potential of science and technology to provide solutions to many of our problems. Photovoltaics can convert the sun's energy into electricity. Hydrogen fuel cells can run non-polluting engines. Yet we have hardly begun to use them, let alone wave-power, wind-power, new insulation techniques and other modern wonders. Why not?

In his book 'The Seventh Enemy', Ronald Higgins outlined the 6 major threats facing us back in the 1970s. The seventh, and deadliest, was the one we are now staring in the face: our own inability to get off our backsides. He was describing apathy, and as I look back on the last 25 years a chill runs down my spine. He was right. Do we now know enough to tackle our apathy, or – more kindly – our institutional inertia?

With help from books like this one, perhaps we do. Yet, as James so neatly puts it, another deadly enemy has emerged since the '70s: the global economy. It destroys the hopes of those environmentalists and others. Its built-in tendency to inequality is, quite simply, genocidal. Even the United Nations is alarmed at the way in which we are being driven to self-destruction by economic forces that put no value on sustainability (let alone on democracy). Its Geo 2000 report lists nine well-established matters of concern, and 3 new ones of 'unprecedented urgency': greenhouse gases, genetically modified organisms, and persistant organic pollutants – all three of which are discussed in these pages.

Tinkering, making 'adjustments', simply aren't enough. We need a total change of direction – towards a benign economy that does not demand growth at any cost. In this little book James Bruges has drawn attention to some specific proposals for achieving sustainability:

• Contraction and Convergence
• The issuing of money by Governments rather than banks
• A Citizen's income
• A four-currency system
• Decision-making at the lowest possible level
• Recognition of a First World Debt
• The World Bank and the IMF to be subject to UN control
• The phasing out of industrial agriculture
• Citizen's juries to assess new technologies
• A stop to the patenting of life forms.

Is it not deeply unfair that in our quickening destruction of the planet it is those who have contributed least to that destruction – the poor and the majority nations – who are already suffering most?

We badly need better leadership. But there is hardly a soul on this planet who is unable to make a contribution, and a million small contributions, as well as the big ideas, will make a million changes. Being part of the solution rather than part of the problem (by, for example, buying organic food) can be hugely satisfying.

And when you want to curse the darkness, remember to light that candle instead.

References

References: general

Global Environment Outlook (GEO 2000). UNEP.
ISBN 1 85383 588 9
Human Development Reports. UNDP (annual)
Royal Commission on Environmental Pollution.
ISBN 0 10 147492 X
State of the World. Worldwatch Institute. (annual)
Tomorrow's World. Friends of the Earth. Earthscan.
ISBN 1 85383 511 0

• Met office Hadley Centre: www.met-office.gov.uk
• US National Oceanic and Atmospheric
Administration: www.noaa.gov
• US Global Change Research Program: www.gcrio.org
• Earth Council: www.ecouncil.ac.cr/
• Rio + 5:
www.ecouncil.ac.cr/rio/focus/report/english/
• Vostok Ice Core data:
http://cdiac.esd.ornl.gov/ftp/trends/co2/vostok.html
• Global Commons Institute : www.gci.org.uk
• New Economics Foundation: www.neweconomics.org
• Rachel's Environment and Health Weekly: This is an
invaluable weekly update on environmental issues:
www.rachel.org
• Turning Point Project: Formed in 1999 specifically to
produce a series of educational advertisements
concerning major issues of the new millennium. These
excellent posters should be prominently displayed in
every school and university. It is being sued by Western
Fuels (a coal federation) for suggesting that fossil fuels
are harming the atmosphere. www.turnpoint.org
• BBC science: http://news.bbc.co.uk/hi/english/sci
• Forum for the Future: www.forumforthefuture.org.uk
• Bradford Peace Studies:
www.brad.ac.uk/acad/peace/home.html
• Going for Green: www.gfg.iclnet.co.uk
• INES, issues of global responsibility:
www.ines2000.org
• Globe Post: www.travelselect.com
• Footprint. www.iclei.org
• Best Foot Forward: http://bestfootforward.com
• Bank of England: www.bankofengland.co.uk
• WWF: www.panda.org
• Citizen's Income Trust: www.citizensincome.org
• Resurgence: www.resurgence.org

- The Ecologist: www.theecologist.org
- New Internationalist: www.newint.org
- Royal Society for the Protection of Birds (RSPB) www.rspb.org.uk

Ethical financial services

- Henderson Investors. SRI team, 3 Finsbury Avenue, London, EC2M 2AP.
- Holden Meeham: www.holden-meeham.co.uk
- Rathbones Ethical Team: www.rathbones.com
- Triodos Bank: www.triodos.co.uk

References: chapters

Unless otherwise stated, information is taken from the book recommended in each section.

Introduction • Full text of the scientists' warning: www.ucsusa.org • The lead editor of the World Bank special report on poverty was also forced to resign, for emphasising the non-income dimension to poverty.

Little Earth • 'She would rather light candles than curse the darkness, and her glow has warmed the world': Adlai Stevenson referring to Eleanor Rooseveldt.

Cod • Information largely taken from Kurlansky's book, The Times colour supplement, and New Internationalist July 2000. • Websites related to the fishing industry: see www.independent.co.uk/links • Further information from WWF.

Don't Predict • The four principles are derived from the four 'System Conditions' of The Natural Step. These were developed by the Swedish oncologist Dr Karl-Henrik Robèrt and achieved consensus among scientists in Sweden. The official wording can be found in 'Playing Safe'. They provide the best working definition of sustainability; most others, such as Brundtland, are so wooly as to be almost meaningless. TNS has organisations in UK, Canada, South Africa, Australia, Sweden, Japan, New Zealand, USA.

Ozone • widely discussed, particularly 'Sharing the World' and the annual Worldwatch Reports.

Carbon and Temperature • The international Vostok study in Antarctica is widely used as the most authoritative source data. It shows that temperature changes have a matching pattern to CO_2 concentrations, see Royal Commission Report Figure 2-V. There are many websites, in particular see www.gcrio.org/ocp98/figure3.html. • See also the Pew Centre in US. The Economist 12.8.00 p81.

CO_2 • World Industrial Product correlation: data from Carbon Dioxide Information Analysis Centre (CDIAC) and World Bank - correlation by Global Dynamics Institute, Rome. • Joint statement by presidents of RS & US.NAS 1992 see full transcription in Rachel's E&HW issue 669. • Prof. Nordhaus box, see Short Circuit p36. **Global Warming** • Multiple sources including UK Met office publications, US Global Research Programme, US Department of Commerce etc. • Also Tyndall Centre, UEA • 'The big picture' based on Global Dynamics Institute, Rome, and

Alberto Di Fazio, theoretical astrophysicist at Astronomical Observatory, Rome. • General background, The Breathing Planet by John Gribbin. • BBC 18.11.99 science website. • IPCC draft report 'Climate Change: Impacts, Adaptation and Vulnerability'. • West Antartic Ice sheet-Nature 393 p325 1998 • Climate Chief's warning: The Independent 23.12.99 • Perverse taxes, see UNDP Human Development Report 1998. • ZeTek, a British company, are building the world's first automated fuel-cell production plant in Cologne, Germany

Europe Cooling • Potsdam Institute: computer model of Atlantic currents. • Scottish Executive's Marine Lab, Aberdeen: measurements of reducing salinity "consistent with models showing the stopping of the pump and the conveyor belt". • Fisheries Lab. of the Faroes: increasing temperature of 'pump' water • Bergen University: Greenland-Norway current into reverse • BBC 25.11 99 science website.

Water • See also aquifers & irrigation: State of the World 2000 ch.3 • disastrous effect of the Narmada dam, see 'The Cost of Living'. Arundhati Roy.

Ecological Footprints • For explanation of Ecological Footprint theory and statistics for different nations see Rio+5 Forum. Wackernanagel & Rees. • See also FoE Environmental Space theory. • For a fuller discussion of Kerala see 'The Growth Illusion' p.310. Also 'Hope Human and Wild' by Bill McKibben.

Inequality • diagram from UNDP Human Development Report 1999 fig 1.6 • US prison population: Washington Post 2.2000.

Weapons of War • General concepts based on Prof Paul Rogers. University of Bradford Department of Peace Studies • Dramatic description of biological warfare danger: see The Economist. 22 January 2000. p57.

Rio and Kyoto • The mantle of criminal GCC denials is being taken over aggressively by Western Fuels Inc., a coal organisation.

How to Make Money • The Economist 22.1.00.

Economic Growth • The Economist 1.1.00 The millennium report 'For the moment the West has triumphed'.

Citizen's Income • Proposals being promoted by the Citizen's Income Trust • Also see 'Instead of the Dole' 1989, an enquiry into integration of the tax and benefits system, by H. Parker. Routledge. Also 'The Economic Consequences of Rolling Back the Welfare State'. 1999, MIT Press, Cambridge & London. • In 'Transforming Economic Life' James Robertson links: 1/ Ecotax reform (a shift of taxation away from employment, incomes and savings, to resource-dependent and environmentally damaging activities). 2/ A tax on land site-values. 3/Citizen's Income.

A New World Order • Douthwaite's strategy is selected because it relates the monetary system to environmental and societal needs with great clarity. A more incremental approach is suggested by James Robertson, who is developing these proposals with the New Economics Foundation.

Them or Us? • Lathur is a project of ASSEFA, (via Action Village India, Shoreditch Town Hall, 380 Old Street, London EC1V 9LT). It is an NGO using Gandhian techniques in Indian villages. • Examples taken from visit and Half Yearly Report 1999 by Mr Arokiasamy • Gandhi quote from 'All Men Are Brothers'. Autobiographical reflections. Continuum 1995 ISBN 0 8264 0003 5. • Similar democratic systems were practised by the Athenians from 507 to 322BC and, of religious groups, by the Quakers. The UK political system is 'elective oligarchy', i.e. government by a small group of people; at both local and national level. See 'An Intelligent Person's Guide to the Classics' by Peter Jones. ch5.

Wealth in Poverty • also The Guardian 27.2.99. • Stan Thekaekara is also working with the UK New Deal for Communities programme of the Social Exclusion Unit of the Cabinet Office, and the Middlesborough project. • see also Nobel economist Amartya Sen's work on comparative wealth.

A Great American Idea • The statement 'whatever happens, whoever is at fault, the wealth of western creditors must be protected and enhanced' was made by Ellen Frank, professor of economics at Boston University, referring to the guiding principle of the IMF and the World Bank.

Third World Debt • special issue: New Internationalist May 1999 • Wolfensohn quote: 'World Bank'. Debt transferred to IMF, and growth of assets from 'Unfinished Business' p7. Update 'An Emerging Scandal' May 2000. All by Jubilee 2000 • US unpaid dues : The Economist 5.8.00 p22.

First World Debt • 'Them or Us' by Andrew Simms when at Christian Aid. • The WTO • Also: FoE The World Trade System: 'Winners and Losers, a Resource Book'; and 'How it works and what's wrong with it'. • FoE. Seattle Series Briefing papers.

Free Trade • Banana dispute: full discussion in Rachel's E&HW No. 679. 9 December 1999 • Logging: The Ecologist. Vol 29 No 6. • Commodity prices: New Internationalist May 99.

Basic Human Needs • See also Maslow's hierarchy of needs • Manfred Max-Neef distinguishes satisfiers (i.e. house) from needs (subsistence), which is useful for development studies. Universidad Austral de Chile; Castilla; 567 Valdivia; Chile, fax (56 63) 212.953

Farming • New concern about synthetic chemicals see Foreword to Global Environment Outlook 2000, by the Secretary-general, Klaus Töpfer • Daffodils: conversation with agent. • 75% costs processing: Understanding Global Issues 97/7

POP • State of the World 2000 • World treaty due to be signed May 2001 see Rachel 703 • analysis of POP disaster see 'Pandora's Poison' by J.Thornton • Pharmaceuticals: see Rachel 702.

Pests and Weeds • see Positive News, Green Futures (Forum for the Future) and Living Earth (Soil Association).

Agrochemical Revolution • We will only confuse kids if we continue to refer to the 'Green Revolution', green now having a totally different connotation • Sumeria barley yields. Cadillac Desert. P261 • US National Academy of Science on GM danger, reported in Rachel issue 695. • Americans for GM labelling: Time Magazine Jan 99 found 81% of Americans want labelling. By the end of the year New York Times 'biotech industry poll' found 93% want labelling.

Microbes • Infection from pigs: The Week 25.3.00. • Most scientists accept that AIDS was transferred from chimpanzees. Edward Hooper, in 'The River' (Penguin), virtually establishes that the transfer was made by an American company experimenting with a polio vaccine called Chat, derived from chimpanzee kidneys, in 1957-60 in the Congo. The company tested Chat on more than a million Africans (the 'patients' did not need a polio vaccine, and a polio epidemic occurred soon after in the vicinity, probably caused by the vaccine). See Matt Ridley, Prospect June 2000. • Another lethal disease with no known cure, from Africa and causing fear in the US, is the 'West Nile Virus' • Also The Economist 15.7.00 p18 and 117.

Antibiotics • See also The Conquest of Disease, Understanding Global Issues 92/2. And 'the doomsday bug', The Week 4.3.2000.

Genes • The Economist 1.7.00.

Population • Based on Professor Abernethy's essay in 'Where Next' edited by Duncan Poore.

Patenting Life • John Moore. Luke Anderson p. 77

Commercial Eugenics • The grammar of the Lee Silver quote has been modified to increase clarity, for original see Rifkin. • See also the work of professor Steven Rose, Brain & Behaviour Research Group, Oxford University. Independent 2 1 2000, i.e. "The sanguine conceit that somehow we have the power to stop or direct evolution is the most arrogant fantasy of all".

Understanding Nature • Intuition • Citizen's Juries: 'Dumbing Down'. Ivo Mosley. Imprint Academic 2000.

Two Japanese Farmers • 'One Bird - Ten Thousand Treasures'. Dr. Mae-Wan Ho. The Ecologist Vol.29 no.6 .

Mental Equipment • For a disciplined exploration of the 'blind' illustration see chapter 8 of 'How the Mind Works' by Pinker (professor of psychology and Director of the Centre for Cognitive Neuroscience at MIT). • Deeper relationships: see 'Care of the Soul' by Thomas Moore. •

A Short Story

of one man's impact *by Alastair Sawday*

James McLean was a modest, practical bass trombonist. When he was 19 he joined the BBC Scottish Symphony Orchestra and nine years later he met Jeannie, a feisty and hard-working marketing professional. Margaret was born three years later and their lives became hectic, as happens when two people juggle careers and child care. There were periods when Jeannie and James hardly saw each other.

Then James discovered a job going with a symphony orchestra in Spain - the break, perhaps, they were looking for. Although neither of them had worked abroad, this seemed a wonderful opportunity to start again in a way that would give them time together as a family. So they took the plunge and emigrated.

For two years they lived in Ronda, then moved to a village called Morenas up in the wooded hills to the north, one hour away from Ronda and five kms away from Castana, the nearby town. Margie settled into the local primary school. They all started to put down roots in the new community.

Now Castana, like so many towns in Spain, had a long musical tradition. For over a hundred years their wind-band had been an important part of the community's life. But the modern world had eroded the town's ability to keep its band going. There were only 19 members, up to 60 years old and all male.

One day in 1993, just four weeks before the Semana Santa (Holy Week) procession in Castana, the town hall asked James to take over the band. Flattered, flustered and feeling hopelessly inadequate to the task, he refused. He never thought of himself as a star. Anyway, 4 weeks was simply not long enough to make any impact. Twice more he was asked, and each time he refused. On the fourth attempt he gave way.

The nineteen players were delightful, bursting with pride and a sense of history, full of energy and conviction. Once he took it on, James was caught – completely. When the great day arrived the band performed with amazing panache. Castana never looked back. James dragooned eight other players from the symphony orchestra to help out and great was the outpouring of enthusiasm. Within three years the band had 70 players, there was a Youth Band of 50, and a music school with 200 students – astonishing in a town of 6,000. Somehow James had pressed a magic button, tapped into a pent-up musical energy.

After their success in Holy Week the band gave a concert in the town and Jeannie has a marvellous video of rows of tiny children, mouths agape. Most of them are now in the band.

In 1996 James, fiercely proud of the band, took them on a tour to Scotland, where they played their hearts out. None of them had been abroad before, so this was a big occasion, to which they rose magnificently. They flew back to Malaga, James bubbling with plans for the future – for a school of music, a symphony orchestra – and catching Jeannie up in his enthusiasm.

The coach drove from Malaga back to Castana, and on the way James, only 35 years old, died suddenly of a heart attack, sitting next to his daughter Margie. The band was devastated, and so was the town. A few days later, 2000 people came to his funeral – one third of the population of Castana.

James had, clearly, worked a special magic among the people of Castana. Jeannie was now determined to take up his baton, and the results are extraordinary: 100 now in the town band and 400 in the school of music, now called 'El Aula Municipal de Musica James McLean'. The school teaches 33 subjects and has 17 teachers. What is more, there is now a Youth Symphony Orchestra too. To cap it all, in the clearest possible demonstration of popular support, the Town Hall has laid the foundations for the new 600-seater theatre to house the town's blossoming cultural programme. This would be astonishing in any city – but Castana is a small town of 6000.

Thus did one man's small, first, gesture let loose a torrent of creative energy. Both he, and Castana, were transformed.

(I have changed all the names, but this is otherwise a true story.)

Alastair Sawday's 'Special Places to Stay' series

Tourism can damage a host culture and its environment. One solution is to support the local economy, especially those who farm organically or serve local food. These much-loved guides encourage such people, and most of our hotels are privately owned, old, buildings run with warmth and humanity. (Our B&Bs certainly are.) We think they are an appealing alternative to what the hotel corporations offer you.

See order form overleaf.

So you've read the book – you now need a holiday!